Elders Lead a Healthy Family

Elders Lead a Healthy Family

Shared Leadership for a Vibrant Church

J. R. Miller

Foreword by Gary L. McIntosh

WIPF & STOCK · Eugene, Oregon

ELDERS LEAD A HEALTHY FAMILY
Shared Leadership for a Vibrant Church

Copyright © 2017 J. R. Miller. All rights reserved. Except for brief quotations in critical publications or reviews, no part of this book may be reproduced in any manner without prior written permission from the publisher. Write: Permissions, Wipf and Stock Publishers, 199 W. 8th Ave., Suite 3, Eugene, OR 97401.

Wipf & Stock
An Imprint of Wipf and Stock Publishers
199 W. 8th Ave., Suite 3
Eugene, OR 97401

www.wipfandstock.com

PAPERBACK ISBN: 978-1-5326-1801-7
HARDCOVER ISBN: 978-1-4982-4319-3
EBOOK ISBN: 978-1-4982-4318-6

Manufactured in the U.S.A.   MARCH 17, 2017

I dedicate this book to my supportive and beautiful wife, Suzanne. In the words of Winston Churchill,

"My most brilliant achievement was my ability to be able to persuade my wife to marry me."

Contents

Foreword

WHEREVER YOU LOOK, WHATEVER you read, or whomever you listen to, it's clear that pastors are hurting, churches are struggling, and ministry is in trouble. Christian and secular writers and researchers report almost weekly that churches are not as fruitful or effective as they were in times past. Such statements are likely overstated to catch attention, but there is a measure of truth in them. Without doubt, those who lead churches in the twenty-first century are facing major changes and challenges.

Church leaders are not standing idly by, nervously twisting their thumbs in anguish over such reports. Instead many, perhaps most, are taking action to turn their churches around and restore vitality where nominality has become normal. To do so, some church leaders are adopting new models of ministry, while others formulate new mission statements. Others are writing long-range plans, while others call people to prayer. Quite a number are engaging their communities in missional activity, while others focus on building a healthy church. However, one common thread flows through nearly all of these efforts to bring back churches to vibrant ministry—leadership.

It is to this issue of biblical leadership that *Elders Lead a Healthy Family: Shared Leadership for a Vibrant Church* is directed. In this book Joe Miller brings to paper his years of research and ministry practice to address questions like: How can we stop pastoral burnout? How can we develop healthier church structures to eliminate isolation? How can we build vibrant churches for the coming generations?

While Miller's answer is simple (see the title)—shared leadership—there are numerous issues to address, which he does in a clear and compelling manner. Readers will appreciate that he builds his ideas on solid biblical exegesis, explores both Old Testament and New Testament passages, and places a premium on character qualities for church leaders. Another plus is that Miller faces head on difficult topics, such as women as elders, women and the pastoral gift, power in leadership, abuse of power in ministry, practicing divine authority, and the pluses and minuses of a CEO church structure. Readers will particularly recognize his gracious and irenic approach. While he argues for an elder/deacon type of church leadership, he does not put down those who choose to use different models of church leadership structure. Instead he cordially invites the reader to consider the biblical evidence and how he or she might apply the insights to their own ministry situations.

Elders Lead a Healthy Family: Shared Leadership for a Vibrant Church is a refreshing look at the larger topic of church leadership, structure, and government. It will challenge your assumptions, attitudes, and perspectives. It is a book I hope will be read by many, but much more than read, I hope its principles and insights will be put into action.

Gary L. McIntosh
DMin, PhD
Professor, Talbot School of Theology, Biola University
La Mirada, CA

Acknowledgments

I AM MOST GRATEFUL for the contributions of the many people who took their time to give me meaningful feedback. Your insight made this book better than what I could ever do on my own. Thank you Christi Cuendet, Dr. Ron Barnes, Lyn Smith, Jennifer Ewing, Cory Marsh, and Wayne Kindie for your editorial insight and friendship.

Introduction

I SAT ACROSS THE table looking into the tired eyes of a long-time friend who was defeated, burned out, and ready to walk away from his church. Steve was the senior pastor of a church that bears all the marks of success, with over 1,400 people in weekly attendance, a fabulous building, dozens of thriving small groups and a selection of qualified leaders who are passionate about serving. With all signs pointing to success . . . why was Steve frustrated to the point of quitting?

In short, Steve is tired of feeling alone. Everyone on staff works for him, is accountable to him, and even though they are friends . . . they are also Steve's employees who need his approval to keep their jobs. Steve sits alone as the head of his church's corporate structure with no equal in whom he can confide his struggles. I'll come back to Steve later, but for now what is clear is that the senior pastor as CEO model of leadership is wearing him out, and in that, Steve is sadly not alone.

While statistics can be abused, the numbers on pastoral burnout are all too obvious. As Paul Vitelli noted in the *New York Times*,

> The findings have surfaced with ominous regularity over the last few years, and with little notice: Members of the clergy now suffer from obesity, hypertension and depression at rates higher than most Americans. In the

last decade, their use of antidepressants has risen, while
their life expectancy has fallen. Many would change jobs
if they could.[1]

So while we could go back and forth debating about the ac-
curacy of the variety of statistical studies, I think most of us can
agree that even the most favorable numbers reflect a problem with
the pastorate in the West.

To help Steve, and those just like him, we must answer the
question "why?" Why does this problem exist and what can we
do to help our leaders? Is the answer to burnout more leadership
books? Executive coaching? Longer vacations and regular sabbati-
cals? etc . . .

No, the answer to pastoral burnout is not found in another
program or another leadership conference. The answer to burnout
is not more coaching or better education.

So what then is the answer?

C. Christopher Smith in his *Christianity Today* article suggests the answer might come from "promoting healthier congregational cultures that do not burn out their clergy, leaders, and
members."[2] Reducing burnout can be accomplished, Smith asserts,
by embracing language that deepens communal ties and by empowering the congregation to do more of the ministry.[3]

Ed Stetzer expresses a similar sentiment in his article that
argues our methodologies must change for churches to remain effective. One of three changes he suggests is the "declergification of
ministry":

> Within our theological understanding of church and
> ordination, let's de-emphasize the role of clergy. Ironi-
> cally, many low church denominationa [*sic*] are not a
> clergy-driven people, but we certainly function like a
> clergy people. Many low church congregations have a
> leadership culture that is essentially a hierarchial priest-
> hood. There's one man who is the only one who has the

1. Vitello, "Taking a Break."
2. Smith, "Koinonia Way."
3. Ibid.

authority to interpret and teach the Bible. To them, the pastor functions almost as an intermediary priest.[4]

Both of these articles offer valuable advice, but fall short in providing a wholistic solution. Changing our terminology and sharing the workload does not address the deeper systemic problems of pastoral leadership. The answer requires our churches dismantle the very structures that foster isolation and burnout. If we hope to save our pastors and build vibrant churches that will reach the next generation, then we need our pastors to abandon the pastor as CEO model of leadership. If we want to preserve our leaders and empower the church, we need a wholesale change in the way we plant, grow, and maintain our churches. Instead of putting a solo leader at the top of Church Incorporated, we need to build teams of elders, doing ministry together, as they lead the family of God.

In the pages to come, I explore what the Bible teaches about shared leadership, elders as the spiritual "big brothers" and shepherds to the family of God. Before we begin our journey, however, I want to provide a few important guidelines for how the Scriptures will be used.

From the beginning, let me assert that putting elders at the helm of a healthy family is not the same as a ministry model. Having a plurality of elders lead does not mean every church in every denomination in every nation will have the same support structures, offer the same opportunities, or utilize the same methods of making disciples. Therefore, the following eight guidelines provide a wonderful summary of how I will apply the teaching of the apostles given to the church. The first seven are quoted from Rodney J. Decker's article "Polity and the Elder Issue."

> 1. Precedence of Doctrinal Passages. Explicit doctrinal passages and commands have precedence over historical narrative. There are many doctrinal passages in Scripture, the specific intent of which is to teach particular doctrinal truth or to require specific action of God's people. There are numerous commands addressed specifically

4. Stetzer, "3 Church Methods."

to the church. In these instances there is little dispute regarding obligation. Such texts must form the primary basis of ecclesiological decisions.

2. Historical Precedence Alone. Historical narrative records what did happen in a given situation. It does not prescribe what must happen in every subsequent situation. Historical precedence alone should never form the basis for antecedence. "On the basis of precedence alone it is probably not valid to say, 'Therefore, one must.'" "Just through being reported as truly happening, no event becomes the revelation of God's universal will."

3. Scriptural Corroboration. Practices based on historical precedence are most clearly normative if corroborated by principles elsewhere in Scripture. There may not be a specific command addressing the situation, but there may well be relevant theological principles which can be established from other prescriptive passages.

4. Noncontradictory. It should be obvious, but for the sake of clarity, a principle claiming support from historical narrative cannot contradict explicit statements found elsewhere in the epistles. "The meaning and principles derived from a story must be consistent with all other teachings of Scripture. A deductive principle drawn from a narrative which contradicts the teaching of some other scriptural passage is invalid."

5. Consistency and Clarity. It is perhaps valid to defend a given practice on the basis of precedence if there is substantial evidence for its practice and that pattern can be demonstrated to be the only pattern present. A consistent and clear pattern must be established. Specifically, polity considerations based on NT example may be valid if the matter is both widespread (the actions of many local churches reflect such a practice) and unique (it is the only way in which the churches did something). "The strongest possible case can be made when only one pattern is found . . . , and when that pattern is repeated within the New Testament itself."

6. Positive versus Negative. In establishing patterns, it must be recognized that positive patterns are clearer than negative patterns. In other words, the fact that something was done is more significant than something that was not done, unless the text explicitly and emphatically states that a specific action was not involved. Arguments from silence are dubious and inconclusive in most instances.

7. Intention Versus Incidentals. Exegesis must emphasize the intention of the passage rather than incidental allusions. Historical narrative texts record numerous minor details. Although accurate descriptions of what actually happened, they are not to be elevated to the primary, didactic level unless the writer is clearly representing these details as significant to his primary thesis. On a related matter, it should be noted that "extensive passages on a subject take priority for theological purposes over brief allusions."[5]

To the above, I would like to add only one more guideline of my own:

8. Principle is destroyed by Law. The error of the Pharisees is that they sought to build a hedge around the Law to keep people from sin. In the age of the Spirit of grace, we must not repeat this error in the name of Jesus. The New Covenant is established by grace alone. There are many valuable principles given to us by the apostles, but any effort to turn a principle of the Spirit into a law of the flesh will destroy the very principle we seek to uphold (Gal 3:2–3; Rom 6:14).

In applying each of these principles, I conclude that when the Scripture does not give clear and specific guidelines, God has allowed for liberty. In passages that speak about elders, the emphasis is almost always on the relationship of elders with the people more than the organization of the church. This does not mean organization is unimportant—it does mean that the Holy Spirit has given the church, and her elders, some discretion in how they choose

5. Decker, "Polity and the Elder Issue," 265–67.

to shepherd the flock in different times and in different cultures. Models of doing ministry are time and culture specific; leading with a plurality of elders is timeless and cross-cultural. With this understanding, let me move into my own experience with leading in a plurality of elders.

1

My Journey from Pastor to Elder

I BEGAN MY DOCTORAL studies at Talbot School of Theology because after ten-plus years of pastoral ministry I felt stagnant in my faith and I hoped that focused study of Scripture would stretch my mind in new directions. As an associate pastor in a church that featured one guy preaching week after week. Quite frankly, I was bored and wanted more. As I studied, prayed, and ministered to the church, God's Spirit began to transform me. God changed the way I dream about leading his family!

I have spent my life participating in the divine community of church. I grew up in the United Methodist tradition, but over the decades I have participated in various others including Evangelical Free, Russian Orthodox, Bible, and various non-denominational/ independent gatherings. I was first ordained in the Christian & Missionary Alliance and have planted two Baptist congregations. I have enjoyed worship among old-school hymn-singing groups, with pew-hopping, rolling-down-the-aisles Pentecostal churches, and everything in between. I have found a home among traditionally black, ethnically Chinese, rural white, and racially integrated church families. In my travels, I have been blessed by the people in the Russian house church, the Romanian Gypsies, the Canadian First Nations, and the Mexican migrant community. I have enjoyed mega, mini, home, rural, and city churches and—amazingly—all of these diverse traditions can, if they so choose, thrive with a plurality of the elders at the helm.

I never imagined the Holy Spirit would use my diverse education and experience to plant not just one, but two, elder-led congregations. In the years since my first church plant in 2005, I have learned much from studying the Scriptures, conversation with good people, and from my many mistakes. Today, as I am planting my second elder-led church, and mentoring the next generation of leaders to plant more, I am convinced that while there are many models for effective church, God's overarching design is to use elder-led families to advance the gospel of Jesus Christ.

In the coming chapters, I endeavor to share what I have discovered about elders in the church. Certainly many others, more qualified and better looking than I, have written on this topic. My only hope is that by adding my small voice to the conversation, God's children will be encouraged to know how "elders lead a healthy family."

2

Our Present Found in the Past

WHEN I TELL PEOPLE that I am one of several elders at my church, one of the first questions I am asked is, "Then who is your pastor?" Other questions I often hear are:

"Who is in charge of your board of elders?"

"If there is no senior pastor in your church, who makes the final decisions?"

"Isn't it better for the church to have only one person to preach and cast the vision?"

These question no longer surprise me, but it does sadden me to realize that so few Christians know what an elder is or how they are called by God to lead his church. In an age when so many are asking why their church leadership does not reflect what they read in their Bibles,[1] it is crucial that people see healthy contemporary examples of elder plurality. In the following pages, I will provide a short history of God's purpose for elders.

Elders Guide God's People

Leadership, structure, and authority have been a part of God's design from Genesis through Revelation. In every age, God has made a place for elders to lead among his people. As we seek to re-discover their Spirit-gifted leadership of God's church, it is helpful

1. Merkle, *Why Elders?*, Kindle loc. 33–35.

to understand the context and culture in which the term "elder" grew. We must move beyond simple dictionary definitions and look at the biblical context in which the term was used. We must all lay aside our contemporary models and mind-sets and examine the unique Jewish context for eldership. In addition to the Jewish tradition, the Apostle Paul established elders in all the Gentile churches he planted. This lets us know that elders were not just a Jewish legacy, but integral to God's plan for leading his church; then and now.

From Moses to the Apostle Paul, elders had a growing and evolving role of leadership among God's people. However, if we hope to peel back the layers of bad tradition and culture, we first need to know who elders were in the Scriptures with a special eye toward their role in the New Testament church.

Elders in the Old Testament

The story of elders begins with the nation of Israel. From ancient times, elders were the older men from each family.[2] In the Pentateuch we read how elders played a key role in the leadership of Egyptians (Gen 50:7), Moabites, Midianites (Num 22:7), and Israelites (Exod 3:16).[3] Elders began as heads of family groups, but later we see how a select group of seventy elders played a more formal role in leading Israel out of Egyptian captivity and toward the promised land (Exod 24:1).[4] The book of Numbers offers a glimpse into the importance God placed on the leadership of Israel's elders.

2. Regarding OT elders being men, Cohn-Sherbok writes, "Evidently, where there are prophets there are also prophetesses. God did not limit his prophetic word to and through men. It is true that seventy elders also prophesied (Num. 11:16–30), but these were all 'men' ('ish' in Hebrew). Though there were prophetesses, there is no evidence that there were any female elders in Israel; when there is any description of elders it is always 'men' as noted above." See Cohn-Sherbok, *Voices of Messianic Judaism*, 161.

3. Wood and Marshall, *New Bible Dictionary*, 305.

4. Ibid.

> Then the Lord came down in the cloud and spoke to him [Moses], and took some of the Spirit that was on him and put it on the seventy elders. And as soon as the Spirit rested on them, they prophesied. But they did not continue doing it. (Num 11:25 ESV)

This passage gives insight into those early days of the Exodus to see how select elders, alongside Moses, were specially equipped by the Spirit of God to govern and rule the people.

The role of elders as leaders among Israel goes well beyond the Exodus. As Wood and Marshall observe:

> After the wilderness period every city seems to have had its own ruling body of elders whose duties, according to Deuteronomic legislation, included acting as judges in apprehending murderers (Dt. 19:12), conducting inquests (Dt. 21:2) and settling matrimonial disputes (Dt. 22:15; 25:7). If theirs was a city of refuge they also heard pleas for asylum (Jos. 20:4; but see also Nu. 35:24).[5]

As the Old Testament story progressed, so too did the role of elders in leading God's family. In line with the Mediterranean culture, elders were first recognized as clan/family leaders. As the population of Israel increased, these family leaders were ordained by YHWH to take on a more complex role of governance as Spirit-empowered national leaders.

Elders in the Synagogue

Fast forward several centuries, and we see how the synagogue, and her elders, played a prominent role in the story of the New Testament. Jesus, throughout his ministry, entered the various synagogues of Palestine to teach.[6] From the earliest days, Paul and his church-planting teams also entered into the synagogues in the Mediterranean region to teach the good news of Jesus.[7] So if we

---

5. Ibid.

6. Matt 12:9; 13:54; Mark 1:21; and Mark 3:1 are just a few examples.

7. A good example of their practice can be found in Acts 13–14. Acts 19

are to understand eldership, it is helpful to know something of the synagogues they helped lead. Where did the synagogue come from and what relationship do her elders have in shaping the elders of the New Testament church?

The full history of the synagogue is shrouded in mystery. The oldest record we have of a synagogue service is found in Luke 4:16ff., where Jesus read the prophet Isaiah and connected it to himself. Beyond the New Testament record, much of the evidence appears centuries after Jesus ascended into heaven and so we cannot accurately impose that knowledge back onto the diverse first-century Jewish communities.[8] The true history of the synagogue is disputed, but most scholars trace its origins to the time of the Diaspora in the sixth through fourth centuries BC following the Babylonian exile. After the temple was destroyed in 586 BC, the synagogue became of place of importance for the Jews scattered among the nations. As time went on, the synagogue grew in influence during the Maccabean period in the second through first centuries BC.[9]

The synagogue was a significant institution that served as the center of civil and religious life for the Jews dispersed among the nations and for those left in Palestine.[10] "The institution of the synagogue was firmly established after the exiles returned to Judea and built meeting places under Ezra's leadership (during which time elders were indispensable)."[11] The purpose of the synagogue was as follows:

- public prayer
- reading of torah
- instruction on civil matters.

---

tells of one instance when they spent three months in a synagogue reasoning with the people to show them that Jesus was the Messiah.

8. Campbell, *Elders*, 45.

9. Ibid., 46.

10. Mappes, "'Elder' in the Old and New Testaments," 90.

11. Ibid.

There were varieties of officials who helped lead the synagogue, including the president, his paid assistant, administrators,[12] various servants, alms collector, messenger and herald but with little evidence that there is any direct correlation to how the elders and deacons in the New Testament church were selected and functioned.[13] Elders were men selected, not by age, but by the power and prestige their families held within the community.[14] In contradistinction to the Christian church whose elders served the spiritual needs of the community, the elders of the Jewish synagogue served only the civil and social needs. The responsibilities of the elders included:

- supervision of proselyte baptisms[15]
- settling disputes and holding court for the people in their region[16]
- presiding over trials and excluding offenders from the synagogue[17]
- representing the community on important social matters.[18]

12. "There are also frequent references to men having been ἄρχοντες, the most general term for administrative officials in the Jewish communities as in the rest of the Greco-Roman world, to people with the title of φροντιστής, γραμματεύς, προστάτης and πατήρ/μητήρ συναγωγῆς. We can only guess for the most part at the responsibilities involved. What is important to note is that all these titles refer to officials with responsibility for the secular concerns of the community as a whole." See Campbell, Elders, 50–52.

13. Miller, "Uniqueness of New Testament Church Eldership," 320.

14. Campbell, Elders, 66. Regarding the notion that synagogue elders were exclusively men, the evidence to the contrary is minimal. "Brooten in particular offers a provocative reassessment of the inscriptional evidence for female leadership in the synagogue, including women elders, among Jews during the Roman and Byzantine periods. But it should be noted that this evidence is rather limited and ambiguous, and it may be that the positions occupied by women were more of an administrative character than of significant authority." Hugenberger, "Women in Church Office," 347.

15. Averbeck, "Focus of Baptism," 275.

16. Scott, "Recent Investigations," 233.

17. Hastings, Dictionary of the Bible, 99.

18. Luke 7:2–5 is one good example where the elders come to Jesus on

Mark 15:1 provides an excellent illustration and insight into how the elders of the synagogue functioned.

> And as soon as it was morning, the chief priests held a consultation with the elders and scribes and the whole council. And they bound Jesus and led him away and delivered him over to Pilate. (Mark 15:1 ESV)

In this story, we see a microcosm of Jewish life ruled by the synagogue. The religious leaders (priests and scribes) and the civil leaders (elders), had Jesus tried, bound and delivered to Pilate. As guardians of the social order, these leaders worked to eliminate the perceived threat to the social and religious order. The elders of the synagogue were ultimately men of power, influence and authority who ruled over the people to keep order in the community.

Elders in Greco-Roman Society

The church of the New Testament was rooted Judaism, but grew in the soil of the Greco-Roman world. Within these two distinct cultures, there is a union in the leadership of those called elders.

> While the term οἱ πρεσβύτεροι is rarely used to describe those in authority, the underlying social patterns are very similar to those of the Jewish world. Although Athenian notions of democracy posed a challenge to their rule, the senior members of well-to-do families continued to wield power and influence at most times and in most places. The usual term for them is οἱ γέροντες, and they are conceptually equivalent of οἱ πρεσβύτεροι in Jewish society and exercise a similar function.[19]

Most notably, elders in the Jewish and Greco-Roman cultures at the time of the first century were men of influence who came from families of power.

---

behalf of an influential centurion proselyte who made significant finical contributions to the synagogue and wanted Jesus to heal his servant.

19. Campbell, *Elders*, 67.

The Roman Senate, the elders of the nation, represented the elite of the elite in society. Spiritual and ethical qualifications were insignificant compared to the perceived social status that elevated these men to positions of leadership. Each man's extended family ties were integral if he hoped to rise to power and influence as an elder of Greco-Roman world.

Elders in the New Testament

During the New Covenant period of Acts, we see the Jewish religious elders in conflict with the apostles (Acts 4:5). Yet despite these conflicts the young church still valued and embraced the role of elder in serving the people of God's new covenant.[20]

The Apostle Paul and the prophet Barnabas were commissioned by the church in Antioch to plant churches among the Gentiles.

> Now there were in the church at Antioch prophets and teachers, Barnabas, Simeon who was called Niger, Lucius of Cyrene, Manaen a lifelong friend of Herod the tetrarch, and Saul. While they were worshiping the Lord and fasting, the Holy Spirit said, "Set apart for me Barnabas and Saul for the work to which I have called them." Then after fasting and praying they laid their hands on them and sent them off. (Acts 13:1–3 ESV)

Called and commissioned to their first missionary journey by the predominantly Jewish church, Paul and Barnabas made sure to appoint elders for each young church in the Gentile region of Galatia.

> When they had preached the gospel to that city and had made many disciples, they returned to Lystra and to Iconium and to Antioch, strengthening the souls of the disciples, encouraging them to continue in the faith, and saying that through many tribulations we must enter the kingdom of God. And when they had appointed elders for them in every church, with prayer and fasting they

20. Acts 11:30; 15:2; 20:17; 21:18.

committed them to the Lord in whom they had believed.
(Acts 14:21–23 ESV)

Similar to the tradition of the Old Testament, a plurality of
elders consistently played a God-ordained role sharing leadership.
However, the uniqueness of the elders in the church compared
to the Jewish counterpart in the OT, the synagogue, and even the
Greco-Roman society cannot be overlooked. As Scott observes,

> while we find abundant evidence of both Jewish elders
> and Christian elders, the latter must not be considered as
> an imitation of the former, because when their position
> and duties are examined they are found to be too dis-
> similar to be the result of such a process.[21]

Elders in the church were not selected based on social status,
power or wealth. In a rejection of cultural expectation, the church
followed the teaching of Jesus and apostolic tradition of selecting
elders based on moral character, sound theology, and the ability
to lead their families in love. The uniqueness of the elders in the
New Testament era to guide the church toward maturity will be
explored in the coming chapters, but for now it is enough to see
that elders were called by God and recognized by the apostles as
essential to the leadership of each congregation.[22]

Elders in the Future Kingdom

As we move beyond the early church in Acts into the future kingdom, the Apostle John's vision from the Lord Jesus shows us that

---

21. Scott, "Recent Investigations," 233–34. See this article for Scott's argument about the uniqueness of deacons in the church: "Kühl urges further
against the Jewish origin of the early church polity the fact, that the deacon, an
officer peculiar to Christians, cannot possibly be traced to the ὑπηρέτης of the
synagogue; for this latter was merely an official of worship, while the former
was active in the whole benevolent life of the congregation. The deacons were
not servants, but were peculiarly endowed men, who had received a special
χάρισμα for their work" (ibid., 235).

22. Merkle, *Why Elders?*, Kindle loc. 225–36.

elders will continue to serve the people of God even in the throne room of YHWH.

> After this I looked, and behold, a door standing open in heaven! And the first voice, which I had heard speaking to me like a trumpet, said, "Come up here, and I will show you what must take place after this." At once I was in the Spirit, and behold, a throne stood in heaven, with one seated on the throne. And he who sat there had the appearance of jasper and carnelian, and around the throne was a rainbow that had the appearance of an emerald. Around the throne were twenty-four thrones, and seated on the thrones were twenty-four elders, clothed in white garments, with golden crowns on their heads. (Rev 4:1–4 ESV)

We read again later in the vision given to John about an elect group of twenty-four elders.

> And the twenty-four elders and the four living creatures fell down and worshiped God who was seated on the throne, saying, "Amen. Hallelujah!" (Rev 19:4 ESV)

From start to finish, Genesis to Revelation, elders have been a part of God's plan. In each period of history, elders have played a unique role, but were called by God to participate in the life of his people. Now, keeping this bit of history in mind, let's focus in on God's plan for elders in the church today.

Elders Today

In stark contrast to the actual history given to us through the Scripture, there are some people who paint a picture of church that functions best without elders. One example is this misleading statement by George Barna and Frank Viola from their book, *Pagan Christianity*.

> The one who plants a first-century-styled church leaves that church without a pastor, elders, a music leader, a Bible facilitator, or a Bible teacher. If that church is planted

well, those believers will know how to sense and follow the living, breathing headship of Jesus Christ in a meeting. They will know how to let Him invisibly lead their gatherings.[23]

This statement is misleading; first, because it paints a false portrait of these Spirit-led communities. From the very beginning, the churches planted by Paul and his coworkers had many false doctrines, conflicts, and disruptions which required the good leadership gifts of both elders and apostles.[24]

Second, it is both historically and biblically incorrect to say that God's ideal church has no elders. From the Jerusalem church and beyond, elders were a part of God's design for a healthy family. As mentioned earlier in the ministry of Paul and Barnabas, the Gentile churches took on a design similar to the church in Jerusalem. As Hort observed in his lectures on the early church:

> Here first we find that these infant communities are each called an Ecclesia, not indeed (so far as appears) from the first preaching, but at least from the second confirmatory visit. Further, Paul and Barnabas follow the precedent of Jerusalem by appointing elders in Jewish fashion (elders being indeed an institution of Jewish communities of the Dispersion as well as of Judaea), and with this simple organisation they entrusted the young Ecclesiae to the Lord's care, to pursue an independent life.[25]

From the beginning of the New Covenant faith established on the cross of our Messiah, elders were a divine part of God's design for leading the church. The role from Old Covenant to New is unique, but there is nothing in the New Testament, or church tradition itself, to suggest that the church today should not embrace these Spirit-gifted leaders among the faithful.

In the next chapter, we will look at some of the key teachings given by the apostles regarding elders and their leadership role in the body of Jesus Christ.

23. Viola and Barna, *Pagan Christianity*, 234.
24. Acts 15:1–41; Gal 2:1–9; and 1 Tim 1:3.
25. Hort, *Christian Ecclesia*, 65–66.

3

A Servant-Team

Elders by Age

THE GREEK TERM FOR elder is "πρεσβύτερος." At its most basic meaning, an elder is a representative of the older generation as compared to the younger (νεανίσκοι).[1] Notwithstanding its unique usage in the Old and New Testaments previously covered, elders (by age) should be respected leaders and role models to those who are younger.

> Do not rebuke an older man (Πρεσβυτέρῳ) but encourage him as you would a father, younger men as brothers, older women (πρεσβυτέρας) as mothers, younger women as sisters, in all purity. (1 Tim 5:1–2 ESV)

The early church had a healthy respect for the elderly. Note here the use of the term πρεσβυτης is used both in the masculine and feminine. Respect for the elder men was certainly a reflection of the shared ethos from both Jewish and Greco-Roman societies.[2] However, it is important to recognize that unlike some other cultures, older women were also highly respected in the church. A special honor was given to those elder-widows who had a long track record of leadership in the church (1 Tim 5:9–10).[3] Providing

1. Kittel et al., *TDNT*, 652.
2. Campbell, *Elders*, 68.
3. Note: "Only in 1 Tim. 5:2 do we find the word presbutéras, the fem. pl.

financial support for strong women who devoted themselves to the ministry and had no other means of support was, and should be today, a hallmark of the church.

But, biblical eldership is more than chronological age!

Elders by Selection

Eldership in the New Testament church described those who were specially selected by the Holy Spirit and empowered to safeguard the church against both false teachers and destructive doctrines.

> Pay careful attention to yourselves and to all the flock, in which the Holy Spirit has made you overseers (ἐπισκόπους), to care for the church of God, which he obtained with his own blood. (Acts 20:28 ESV)

This passage introduces a new Greek term often translated "overseer" or "bishop," but we will see later in this chapter, this term is used as a functional synonym with the Greek terms "πρεσβυτης." For now, it is most important to note that all elders (by age) are worthy of honor, but elders chosen to teach and preach the gospel of Jesus Christ were worthy of even higher regard from the church.

> Let the elders (πρεσβύτεροι) who rule well be considered worthy of double honor, especially those who labor in preaching and teaching. (1 Tim 5:17 ESV)

And if, at any time, an elder was acting in a manner that did not match his position of authority he was to be reprimanded and/or removed from his office.

> For the Scripture says, "You shall not muzzle an ox when it treads out the grain," and, "The laborer deserves his wages." Do not admit a charge against an elder except on the evidence of two or three witnesses. As for those

---

acc. of presbúteros (4245), elder, meaning female elders. However, there the reference is not to women elders of the church, but rather to older women which is the literal meaning of the word." See Zodhiates, *Complete Word Study Dictionary*, s.v. "πρεσβύτερος." See also Schweizer, "Ministry in the Early Church," 839.

who persist in sin, rebuke them in the presence of all, so
that the rest may stand in fear. In the presence of God
and of Christ Jesus and of the elect angels I charge you
to keep these rules without prejudging, doing nothing
from partiality. Do not be hasty in the laying on of hands,
nor take part in the sins of others; keep yourself pure.
(1 Tim 5:18–22 ESV)

Unlike the surrounding cultures, social status and wealth
could not preserve an elder's role as leader. His character and cor-
responding choices alone would determine his place in the church.
An elder was to receive the wages of his actions. If he ruled well,
the church was to support him. If he failed to rule well, his wages
were to be his public discipline. The failure to discipline an elder
was akin to participation in their sin. Therefore, both the selection
and dismissal of an elder was never to be taken lightly.

Elders Are Men

"Should women be elders appointed to lead the church?" I wres-
tled with this issue for more than a decade and there are three
arguments in favor of the answer "yes."

First, throughout my life, I have served alongside many amazing women—including my own wife—who were highly gifted by
God to lead the church. Years ago when my wife and I were planting
our first church, we tried to connect with a popular church-planting
group based in Seattle because of their emphasis on eldership.

At the time we approached this group, my wife, Suzanne, and
I had been married for more than a decade and had done ministry together for even longer. We knew well each other's strengths
and weaknesses and had found strength in serving the church as
a married couple.

Together, we went through the interview process, took the
assessment, and together we walked into the room of five men,
the elders who were responsible to oversee the process, and who
would give us the results.

"Everything looks good, but we do have one concern," said Jeremy.

Jeremy was their newest elder, younger than me, recently married, but had never led in a church. He gave us the results of their assessment.

"If you want to have a healthy marriage while leading a church, you need to stay within your God-ordained roles as husband and wife."

I was not sure what he was talking about, but Jeremy continued.

"If you want to partner with our group, your wife needs to step down from leadership, stay home, take care of the kids and make sure to serve your needs" (a euphemism in this group for keeping me sexually satisfied).

Now my wife loves being home with our kids, but in our church plant she was fulfilling her call and using her giftings to serve the church. To simply dismiss her as a leader and say she must stay home reflects the kind of discrimination against women leaders, verging on misogyny, that really angered me. If this is what it meant for men to be elders, I did not want any part in this group.

The second argument in favor of having women as elders is a cultural consideration. We live in a culture that is open to women in leadership and that makes it far more socially persuasive to answer this question in the affirmative. Ben Witherington, a scholar I highly respect, makes this argument from culture.

> Sometimes you hear the argument that since it is assumed in 1 Timothy that the elders will be men who are faithful to their one and only wives, that this must signal that only men should be elders in churches. This is totally forgetting that Paul is speaking as a missionary into a strongly patriarchal cultural setting whether in Ephesus or on Crete, and his principle is to start where the people already are, not where he would like them to be. This means starting with the existing male leadership structure in the culture until the leaven of the Gospel can fully do its work and change things from the inside out. So quite naturally, it is men that Timothy and Titus are going to appoint first as leaders to these brand new

church plants. This does not mean it needs always and forever to be that way, but the new converts would have to be convinced by loving persuasion that it was o.k. for women to fill such roles.[4]

Witherington's basic point seems to be that Paul restricts eldership to men in these early church plants, but only as a concession to the patriarchal culture. And, even though Jesus and Paul are very countercultural in their views on women in leadership,[5] when it came to appointing elders, they just could not push that boundary so they waited, planted seeds, and hoped that someday the church would change. Well, culture has radically changed in the last two thousand years and I certainly want my wife to be valued for all that she does and I want all women in every church who are gifted by the Spirit to be taken seriously as respected leaders.

Third, there has been significant advancement in biblical scholarship in recent decades (especially in the area of rhetorical analysis) and this has helped men like Kenneth E. Bailey create a compelling case for women as elders. In his well written article from the early 1990s, he concludes:

> In summary, the NT has clear cases of women disciples, teachers, prophets and deacons/ministers. We have near certitude in perceiving Junia to be a female apostle. It is possible to see female elders in 1 Tim. 5:2. Thus women appear on nearly all, if not all, levels of leadership in the NT Church.[6]

4. Witherington, "Why Arguments Against Women."

5. Witherington makes this very argument in various writings. He demonstrates how Jesus' treatment of women was radically countercultural in his work "Women in the Ministry of Jesus," 22ff. He also writes of Paul, "Paul is indeed seeking to inculcate a minority or counter-cultural ethic," see Witherington, *1 and 2 Thessalonians*, 118. So it strains credulity to conclude that in this one area of leadership, Paul would now turn his back on what he believed a necessary foundation of equality in the church. In this instance, it seems Witherington's hermeneutic is less consistent and more convenient.

6. Bailey, "Women in the New Testament," 212. Alastair Campbell also notes the following: "A number of Jewish inscriptions, admittedly all later than our period, show women holding office in the Jewish communities. There was then probably no one attitude to women in the earliest churches either, and it

This understanding is shared by some interpreters who see the feminine use of πρεσβυτης in 1 Tim 5:2 as female elders.[7] In addition, there are a variety of traditions over time that have accepted both male and female eldership in the church.[8]

Without question, Paul and the early church recognized that women were empowered by God to help lead the church. And, just like men, Paul encouraged the church to give financial support to those women who dedicated their lives to serving. Consequently, Christian women took on leadership roles with few parallels in the first century world. As Campbell notes,

> There is no reason to doubt that such women were able to "contribute significantly to the spread of Christianity in the early years of its expansion," or that Paul's approach in this matter was deliberate, unusual, and "resulted in the elevation of women to a place in religious work for which we have little contemporary parallel."[9]

For these three reasons, I would prefer to answer the question, "Should women be elders appointed to lead the church?" in the affirmative. However, even after prayerful consideration of these arguments I find them wanting. I am still not able to make the leap to accept female elders over the clear instruction given by Paul that elders in the church were to be men of special character.

---

could change over time in response to changing pressures. Opportunities for women to lead the churches probably did become fewer in the generation after Paul's death." See Campbell, *Elders*, 127.

7. See the arguments presented in the following: Bailey, "Women in the New Testament," 2; Keener, *IVP Bible Background Commentary*, 1 Tim 5:1–2; and Bates, "Gender Ontology and Women," 6–12. In response, you can review Lewis, "'Women' of 1 Timothy 3:11," 188ff.

8. The Shakers are just one example where "two male and two female elders in every fully organized community or family in each society, having charge of its spiritual affairs, and two deacons and two deaconesses subordinate to the elders and having charge of the temporal concerns." Jackson, *New Schaff-Herzog Encyclopedia*, 190. See also a discussion of the Council at Laodicea in the 4th century, which banned female elders due to the popularity and perceived abuse of placing women in this role: Charteris, "Woman's Work," 288.

9. Campbell, *Elders*, 138. See also Brown, *Analytical Exposition*, 585.

> Therefore an overseer (ἐπίσκοπον) must be above reproach, the husband of one wife, sober-minded, self-controlled, respectable, hospitable, able to teach. (1 Tim 3:2 ESV)

and

> This is why I left you in Crete, so that you might put what remained into order, and appoint elders (πρεσβυτέρους) in every town as I directed you—if anyone is above reproach, the husband of one wife, and his children are believers and not open to the charge of debauchery or insubordination. (Titus 1:5–6 ESV)

In every case where someone is instructed to appoint elders, the context makes it clear that men alone are to fill that role. The clarity of the Scripture cannot be overcome by the force of the three arguments presented above.

First, even though men alone can serve as elders, the alternative isn't that women must stay home. There is a spectrum of ministry opportunities between these two black-and-white options. Telling women the only job they have is to stay home, raise kids and have sex with their husband is a cultural bias and not a biblical directive. That being said, nor should we diminish the great calling on women, like my wife, who also chose to stay home. These stay-at-home moms are in God's eyes great leaders in the church and play an invaluable role by raising up the next generation of disciples.

Second, even though men are elders, this role should not be confused with "leader," "minister," or even "pastor." There are many kinds of leaders in the church and following the biblical guideline on male eldership does not in any way invalidate the role of women as valued leaders in the church. These first two arguments are really built on a flawed view of ministry that I will address later in the book. For now, I want to move forward by addressing the third argument of cultural concession by Paul.

Third, Paul was never afraid to challenge the culture if it was counter to the gospel. We see how the church easily broke from the synagogue and Greco-Roman tradition of letting wealth determine who could be an elder. So there is no foundation to accuse him of pandering to patriarchal expectations in these passages when he has in so many other passages challenged the status quo.

Leadership Is *Not* Power

The conclusion that the role of elder is reserved for men must not be misconstrued—this is not primarily a debate about Egalitarian vs. Complementation. To say women are not to serve as elders should in no way diminish their divine call to lead, preach, teach, disciple, and breath life into God's family. As John A. Jelinek writes in the *Journal on Ministry and Theology*,

> God's appointment of the man as leader in the local church has nothing to do with a want of leadership ability on the part of any woman. There is no implicit or explicit ontological or soteriological superiority or inferiority implied in Paul's directive toward divinely appointed roles for men and women.[10]

Confusion comes in because in our culture "leadership" has become synonymous with "power" and the natural conclusion is that the exclusion of women from eldership is an elevation of men above women—this is a dangerous and wrong conclusion.

Leadership in much of the church has become a code word for power—and that is a disastrous abuse of Scripture. The problem is that in response to corrupt leadership (leadership = power), we have turned to other unhealthy leadership models (no leaders = shared power *or* men in power = women in power). But in each of these cases, leadership is still being defined by its use, or nonuse, of "power." Leadership in the church has been redefined

---

10. Jelinek, "Annotations," 160. Please note, Jelinek seems to use this term "leadership" as a synonym for pastor/elder. This conflation of the two words should not be misconstrued as my viewpoint and I lay out the distinction later in this book. However, his larger point that different roles do not necessitate a diminished value are an important foundation for our understanding of the biblical teaching on eldership as reserved for men.

by worldly standard of control instead of refined by biblical standard of mutual submission.[11]

Clarity comes instead when we treat biblical eldership as a Spirit-led demonstration of wisdom, love, joy, maturity, and peacemaking. Women today, as they did in the NT church, can lead and teach in the church. As Bailey rightly points out,

> As a deacon/minister of the church in Cenchreae, Phoebe surely exercised some form of authority over men. Priscilla had theological authority over her student Apollos. The women prophets naturally carried the authority which their message gave them. Lydia is prominent in the founding of the church in Philippi.[12]

Women who are gifted by the Spirit can teach, pastor,[13] and lead in the church, but the specific office of elder is reserved for men. This diversity of ministry, should never be interpreted as inequality.

As a trained engineer, I think there is a lesson here we can learn from math.[14] In a school somewhere around the globe, right now, there is a kid asking himself, "Where will I ever use this stuff in real life?"

The answer is—church!

---

11. Adapted from my article "Feminism."

12. Bailey, "Women in the New Testament," 127.

13. The same hermeneutic that leads me to conclude only men are elders leads me to conclude that women are gifted by the Spirit as pastors in the church. However, this does not mean we need to accept the world's view that men and women are the same. . . . they are not. Both men and women are created in the image of God and both are needed to reflect the fullness of his glory. The reason God created men and women is because each sex has unique qualities that are necessary to be the church. So while women and men can both have a pastoral gifting, that does not mean they both function the same way in the church. Acknowledging the high call God has placed on women to help lead in the church does not mean we have to blur the distinctive beauty between the sexes. See my article "Women and the Pastoral Gift."

14. Miller, "Algebra in the Church."

When it comes to math and faith, algebra can teach us about relationships and roles we play as both men and women in leadership.

So let's start with a simple algebraic equation:

$$a + b = c + d$$

In this equation we can see the life of the church and family. On each side of the equation we have the unique functions (a, b, c, d). Each part brings something unique, but added together they remain equal in value.

In the Church:

Elder + Elder = Sheep + Sheep

Leader = Follower

In Life:

Man = Woman

Rich = Poor

In the Family:

Father = Daughter

Wife = Husband

Brother = Sister

Mother + Father = Son + Daughter

God has created and equipped us for a diversity of roles within the church and within our families. We must learn to embrace our differences rather than normalize them. Mothers have authority over their sons but each person is equal in value and purpose in the kingdom of Jesus. The husband is the head of the wife yet they remain equal in worth to their families and to God. Elders have authority over the flock but each person is equal in value and purpose to the life of the church. The giftings of the Spirit and our natural talents set us apart for unique service to the Lord, but the

shed blood of Jesus Christ unites us and makes us equal at the foot
of the cross.

There is a lot we can learn from using algebra in the church
to ensure that leadership is less about wielding power and more
about servanthood and mutual submission.

Elders Are Mature Big Brothers

Not just any man can be an elder. Eldership demands demonstration of maturity. Mature elders live life in front of the church as the
older brother. I use this term "big brother" here in context of both
Jesus' teaching and in contrast to the Roman Catholic tradition of
priest as "father" and pope as "holy father."[15]

The Roman Catholic Church used the terminology of priest as
"father" to create a hierarchy in the church and a division between
priest and people. Jesus, in stark contrast, said that the church was
to live as a gathering of brothers and sisters with only one Father,
who is God. The Apostle Matthew records for us the following:

> While he was still speaking to the people, behold, his
> mother and his brothers stood outside, asking to speak
> to him. But he replied to the man who told him, "Who
> is my mother, and who are my brothers?" And stretch-
> ing out his hand toward his disciples, he said, "Here
> are my mother and my brothers! For whoever does the
> will of my Father in heaven is my brother and sister and
> mother." (Matt 12:46–50 ESV)

In this brief exchange we discover the heart of God that elders
must serve as the big brothers of God's family and lead each individual into relationship with our heavenly Father.

Across cultures and times, it seems inherent to mankind's
thinking that "brother" is reserved for an equal and "father" for
a superior.[16] Reflecting both that common understanding and the

---

15. Thein, *Ecclesiastical Dictionary*, 684.

16. Barton, "Salutations," 107. Barton notes, "Most of the letters from the
time of the Neo-Babylonian and early Persian empires (c. 550–450 b.c.) are
somewhat more elaborate. An equal is addressed as 'brother,' a priest as 'father.'"

teaching of Jesus, the apostles saw themselves as brothers to all the saints in every church (2 Pet 3:15; Rev 1:9). The saints of the New Testament church recognized each other as brothers and sisters; each person gifted uniquely by the spirit to serve the good of all—yet in their diversity there persisted a divine equality. Leaders in the church were not "fathers" . . . there is only one Father who is God. Leaders in the church were brothers and sisters, called to a place of authority based on maturity of faith and demonstration of service. Francis Schaeffer captures the heart of Jesus well in his book *No Little People, No Little Places*:

> Again, Jesus said, "But be not ye called Rabbi; for one is your Master, even Christ, and all ye are brethren" (Matt. 23:8). This does not mean there is to be no order in the church. It does mean that the basic relationship between Christians is not that of elder and people, or pastor and people, but that of brothers and sisters in Christ. This denotes that there is one Father in the family and that his offspring are equal. There are different jobs to be done, different offices to be filled, but we as Christians are equal before one Master. We are not to seek a great title; we are to have the places together as brethren.[17]

The early church knew nothing of elders as father.[18] However, as the church grew, the sibling relationship was replaced with an institutionalized relationship of power and control. As Carl F. H. Henry laments,

> As medieval Christianity became institutionalized and the ecclesiastical hierarchy declared sacraments to be salvific, the experience of God's fatherhood was pushed more and more into the background. The priest as father, and the pope as father of fathers, rather than God

17. Schaeffer, *Complete Works*, 10.

18. It is noteworthy that Paul does refer to Timothy as his true son in the faith (1 Tim 1:2). and some have derived from this the idea that elders are fathers. However, this reads into the text an hierarchical relationship that is not intended by Paul. Paul's writings nowhere establish an office of "father," but instead emphasized a relationship of loving care between two men who shared a special bond of kinship.

as Father and Christ as great high priest, came to hold center stage.[19]

This is an important reminder of how we must experience elders. In God's church, elders are not a special class of Christian held to a higher standard of morality or service. Elders are not the "clergy" and everyone else the "laity."[20] Elders are the spiritual big brothers who model the maturity and devotion to the family that every sibling should strive to emulate.

> Just as Paul could say, "Be imitators of me as I am of Christ" (1 Cor. 11:1; cf. 2 Tim. 3:10–11), and just as he could command Timothy to "set the believers an example in speech and conduct, in love, in faith, in purity" (1 Tim. 4:12), and just as he could tell Titus, "Show yourself in all respects a model of good deeds and in your teaching show integrity, gravity, and sound speech that cannot be censured" (Titus 2:7), so the pattern is to be continued in the lives of all church leaders today. It is not optional that their lives be examples for others to follow; it is a requirement.[21]

As big brothers, each younger brother and sister is expected to model the behavior of the mature "older sibling." The elder walks in such a way that each and every member of the family can emulate their dedication to Christ.

Elders Are Mature in Faith

The role of elder is not about chronological age, but maturity of faith. While a case can be made by tradition for restricting eldership

---

19. Henry, *God, Revelation, and Authority,* 6:320.

20. Certainly there are some who make this argument that there must be a distinction made between clergy and laity and they attempt to draw this distinction from the earliest days of the New Testament church through the tradition of the early church fathers. While I find this argument lacking, it is presented in some length by Hodge, "Review of Theories," 467ff.

21. Grudem, *Systematic Theology,* 918–19.

to men over the age of thirty,[22] there is no biblical guideline to support this practice. That being understood, the church in recent decades has been all too willing to allow young men who lack maturity, doctrinal wisdom, and experience that comes from age, to lead the church. Ed Glasscock offers some wise counsel in this area.

> In many churches today men are placed into positions of pastor or elder based on education, personality, or professional achievements. However, the Bible does not consider any of these. In the Scriptures an elder was an older, mature adult who was recognized for his wisdom and experience. He was to be looked up to for advice and guidance. His character, not his achievements, was important.[23]

Elders were not hired into service based on their resume of achievement, ability to preach, draw a big crowd, or academic prowess. Rather, they were selected predominantly, but not exclusively,[24] from within the local family based on their recognized history of faithful service to God, doctrinal integrity, and proven character.[25] They were role models for what the young in faith should aspire to become. But, without question, the "most important qualification emphasized in the New Testament is the evidence of the Holy Spirit in the life of each man."[26]

---

22. Glasscock, "Biblical Concept of Elder," 70.

23. Ibid., 67.

24. In contrast to Paul's practice of appointing elders in Acts 15 at the end of his first missionary journey, Timothy is one notable exception as he appears to have been appointed and brought in by Paul to a local church to help restore her to health.

25. Some have read this to mean that an elder must first start off as a deacon and once they prove themselves can then move into the office of elder. While this may happen, these roles are filled by people who have a different calling and gifting from the Holy Spirit. This thinking stems from the Western business mind-set that sees these unique roles as hierarchical: men advancing from one "lower" job into a new "higher" job. Deacon is not a stepping-stone to elder. Each is a unique and valued ministry in the family and should be treated as such.

26. Glasscock, "Biblical Concept of Elder," 70.

Observing how a man serves over a length of time is important. I know this to be true from personal failure. When I planted my first church, I was excited to live out the vision of a plurality of elders guiding the family. I was so ready to be done with the senior pastor as CEO model of ministry that I allowed my enthusiasm to override my reason. Not wanting to lead alone, I selected three men whom I had known for a long time, but never observed in ministry, to serve with me as elders. Again, these were good friends, but men I had not observed firsthand leading others. I knew they had a heart to serve, so I reasoned I could train them, "on the job" to help lead. I was wrong. Within a year, all three men left the church and I was left alone to clean up the confusion. Let me tell you from firsthand experience, there is nothing more detrimental to a young church plant than having three of the four elders quit.

Friendship is not enough. Being good men of character is not enough. It takes time to observe a man's works, both good and bad, before he is given the reigns of leadership. Accordingly, Paul warns Timothy that he should never be hasty to select elders.

> The sins of some people are conspicuous, going before them to judgment, but the sins of others appear later. So also good works are conspicuous, and even those that are not cannot remain hidden. (1 Tim 5:24–25 ESV)

Take your time. Don't rush to appoint elders. Wait until you have observed a man walking in maturity, who is not a slave to sin, and demonstrates the fruit of good works in his life and is respected as a leader in the church.

Elders in Community

Elders were not men selected to serve as the solo head of a church. Once again the terminology of "big brothers" serving the family gives us a healthy picture of the mature siblings working together to guide the family according to the will of God the Father. Note how in 1 Peter 5:1 the Apostle Peter exhorts the elders—plural—to shepherd the church in the name of our one Shepherd Jesus Christ. Elders are always addressed as a plurality . . . never as individuals.[27]

- Acts 11:30 . . . elders
- Acts 14:23 . . . when they had appointed elders
- Acts 15:2–4 . . . apostles and elders
- Acts 15:6, 22, 23 . . . apostles and elders
- Acts 20:17, 28 . . . elders of the church . . . overseers
- Philippians 1:1 . . . overseers and deacons
- 1 Thessalonians 5:12–13 . . . those (plural) who have charge
- 1 Timothy 5:17 . . . elders who direct the church well
- Titus 1:5 . . . appoint elders in every city
- Hebrews 13:7, 17, 24 . . . leaders
- James 5:14 . . . call for the elders
- 1 Peter 5:1–3 . . . elders.

Each elder is a man selected to function in both communion and concert alongside the other elders. Glasscock makes a key observation that "elders did not function individually, as did the prophets, but were always seen as a college or council."[28]

The New Testament ideal is for a plurality of elders to share the mantle of leadership. I think back to my friend Steve, frustrated as he sips his coffee and ready to call it quits. The truth is, he is a victim of his own success in a model of leadership that demands one person sit alone at the top of the leadership pyramid. It takes a certain personality that enjoys that kind of power to lead alone, and that is why elders must be selected based on their ability to work with others, share leadership, and demonstrate a humility to submit their own desires to the council of wise leadership (1 Tim 4:14).

27. Mounce, *Pastoral Epistles*, 46:163.
28. Ibid.

Elders Are Servants

The New Testament uses two words, elder (πρεσβύτερος) and overseer/bishop (ἐπίσκοπος), as functional synonyms to describe the same group of church leaders.[29] As John R. W. Stott points out, these two words are rooted in the unique Jewish and Roman influence on the early church. Stott observes, "Luke called them πρεσβύτεροι ('elders'), a word borrowed from the Jewish synagogue (Acts 20:17), while Paul called them ἐπίσκοποι ('overseers or guardians'), a word borrowed from a Greek context (v. 28). The two titles evidently described the same people."[30] Considering this history, it is fair to say that each term was used to emphasize a unique quality of eldership.

Servants like Christ

Without a doubt, the most important reference to elder comes in 1 Peter, where Jesus himself is described as our shepherd/overseer:

> [Jesus] himself bore our sins in his body on the tree, that we might die to sin and live to righteousness. By his wounds you have been healed. For you were straying like sheep, but have now returned to the Shepherd and Overseer (ἐπίσκοπον) of your souls. (1 Pet 2:24–25 ESV)

In accordance with this passage, elders are earthly representatives of the one true elder, Jesus Christ, who is the shepherd and overseer of our souls. Christ Jesus alone is our senior pastor (1 Pet 5:4). The imagery is powerful when we recognize that some men are uniquely ordained by the Spirit to be Christ's under-shepherds to the church.

---

29. Note, Mounce writes, "Although eventually the overseer/bishop was elevated above the elders/presbyters and the two terms ceased referring to the same group (see Form/Structure/Setting on 1 Tim 3:1–7), there is clear evidence from the early church that originally both titles described the same office." See Mounce, *Pastoral Epistles*, 308.

30. Stott, "Ideals of Pastoral Ministry," 68. Adapted from the original, Stott, "Christian Ministry in the 21st Century," 4.

Servants Who Love

Each term, elder (πρεσβύτερος) and overseer/bishop (ἐπίσκοπος), works in concert to describe a man who is a loving servant to the church.

> A dispute also arose among them, as to which of them was to be regarded as the greatest. And he said to them, "The kings of the Gentiles exercise lordship over them, and those in authority over them are called benefactors. But not so with you. Rather, let the greatest among you become as the youngest, and the leader as one who serves. For who is the greater, one who reclines at table or one who serves? Is it not the one who reclines at table? But I am among you as the one who serves." (Luke 22:24–27 ESV)

Jesus does not reject the role of leaders, or authority, in the church, any more than he could reject his own role as Messiah. What Jesus does so well is redefine a leader as someone quite different from the world's kind of leader. Jesus is the head, yet he chose to serve (Phil 2:1–10). Elders are gifted to lead, but they must model the life of Jesus by loving the church. In his book *The Biblical Foundations of Christian Worship*, the late Robert Webber paints a vivid picture of the elder/bishop.

> "Elder" and "bishop," then, are synonymous, but whereas "elder" indicates the great dignity surrounding this office, "bishop" signifies its function of rule or oversight. In the New Testament oversight is especially related to the figure of the shepherd, who feeds and cares for his flock. It is therefore natural that pastoral language is interwoven with the use of the terms overseer and bishop (Acts 20:28; cf. John 21:15–17). In their pastoral oversight of congregational life, elders reflect Christ's own office as the shepherd and bishop of souls (1 Pet. 2:25; cf. John 10:11–16; Heb. 13:20; 1 Pet. 5:4).[31]

---

31. Webber, *Biblical Foundations of Christian Worship*, 172.

In every major passage that talks about eldership, there is a consistent emphasis upon the task of caring for the spiritual well-being of the church. As Elwell observes,

> The elders' task of oversight and discipline can be described in terms of keeping watch and shepherding on behalf of the great shepherd Jesus Christ. In Paul's farewell to the Ephesian elders he said: "Keep watch over yourselves and all the flock of which the Holy Spirit has made you overseers. Be shepherds of the church of God, which he bought with his own blood" (Acts 20:28).[32]

Primarily, the elder is a spiritual "big brother" who demonstrates the love of Christ to the entire church. The elder is the mature sibling to his "younger" brothers and sisters who guides the Father's kids into holiness. Consider the Apostle Peter's instruction on the subject:

> So I exhort the elders among you, as a fellow elder and a witness of the sufferings of Christ, as well as a partaker in the glory that is going to be revealed: shepherd the flock of God that is among you, exercising oversight, not under compulsion, but willingly, as God would have you; not for shameful gain, but eagerly; not domineering over those in your charge, but being examples to the flock. And when the chief Shepherd appears, you will receive the unfading crown of glory. Likewise, you who are younger, be subject to the elders. Clothe yourselves, all of you, with humility toward one another, for "God opposes the proud but gives grace to the humble." (1 Pet 5:1–5 ESV)

Paul, and his fellow apostles, modeled this very attitude among the churches. Even under great distress, the apostles did not rely on their divine apostolic authority to control the church. They could have used their office to demand obedience. They could have used their authority to keep the people in line. Instead, the apostles chose to use the power of relationship.

> For we never came with words of flattery, as you know, nor with a pretext for greed—God is witness. Nor did

32. Van Dam, "Elder," 198.

we seek glory from people, whether from you or from others, though we could have made demands as apostles of Christ. But we were gentle among you, like a nursing mother taking care of her own children. So, being affectionately desirous of you, we were ready to share with you not only the gospel of God but also our own selves, because you had become very dear to us. For you remember, brothers, our labor and toil: we worked night and day, that we might not be a burden to any of you, while we proclaimed to you the gospel of God. You are witnesses, and God also, how holy and righteous and blameless was our conduct toward you believers. For you know how, like a father with his children, we exhorted each one of you and encouraged you and charged you to walk in a manner worthy of God, who calls you into his own kingdom and glory. (1 Thess 2:5–12 ESV)

Instead of force, the apostles persuaded people through their labor of love. This is what it means for elders to rule well. Leading like Jesus did—laying down his life and sacrificing everything—is what real power looks like in the church.

Now insofar as the elder models loving-sacrifice and moral character, his service is a demonstration of the ethic every disciple should aspire to.

Servants Who Model Christ

There are some aspects of servant-shepherding that are common to both the elders and every disciple of Jesus. The elder should be mature in all of these and inspire the flock to follow in their example.

- The elders administer relief to those in need—Acts 11:29, 30.

- The elders model a Christ-like leadership over those in their charge—1 Pet 5:3.

- The elders keep the church rooted in sound doctrine—Acts 15:4, 6, 23.

- The elders who are properly gifted should both teach and preach the gospel—1 Tim 5:17.
- The elders protect the flock from the wolves who would ravage her—Acts 20:28.
- The elders minister to the sick and pray for healing—Jas 5:14, 15.

However, there are also unique aspects of leadership that are reserved for the office of elder.

Servants Who Rule Well

Elders have a distinct responsibility to lead the church. Three aspects of ruling well are as follows:

- Elders mentor and appoint other elders in younger congregations—Titus 1:5.
- Elders rule well over the congregation—1 Tim 5:17.
- Elders ensure right doctrine is passed on—2 Tim 2:2.

In our own church plant, this means that we have a regular flow of interns whom our elders mentor with the hopes of sending them out to plant new churches. We lead not just to grow our own congregation, we lead to grow other congregations who will embrace the vision of shared leadership under the plurality of elders.

Now that we have seen how a biblical elder rules, we can move on to examine how the Spirit uses spiritual gifts to empower elders for their service.

4

Elders Are a Gift from God's Spirit

THE TOPIC OF "SPIRITUAL gifts" is not without its own controversy, but I think it is probably one of the most important for understanding the role of elders in the church.

Elder Is More Than a Title

In nearly every church in the West, there is a leader that everyone calls "pastor." In Scripture, however, the word "pastor" is not used as a title of human leadership, but as a description of *how* the Holy Spirit has gifted some to lead.

> And he gave the *apostles*, the *prophets*, the *evangelists*, the *shepherds* (ποιμένας) and *teachers, to equip the saints for the work of ministry*, for *building up* the body of Christ, until we all attain to the *unity* of the faith and of the *knowledge* of the Son of God, to *mature* manhood, to the measure of the stature of the *fullness of Christ*, so that we may *no longer be children*, tossed to and fro by the waves and carried about by every wind of doctrine, by human cunning, by craftiness in deceitful schemes. Rather, *speaking the truth in love*, we are to *grow up in every way* into him who is the head, into Christ, from whom the whole body, *joined and held together* by every joint with which it is *equipped*, when *each part is working*

properly, makes the body *grow* so that it *builds itself up in love.* (Eph 4:11–16 ESV, emphasis added)

Most striking in this passage is that the apostles, prophets, evangelists, shepherds, and teachers mentioned here are descriptive of a ministry not an office. Look again at each of the highlighted words in the passage. Each one emphasizes the purpose of these foundational ministries is to build up the church into a strong family. And how is this ministry accomplished? Every member must be equipped. These five foundational ministries are given as giftings from the Holy Spirit so that in turn every believer can use their Spirit-gifting to grow the body into maturity.

The "shepherd" then is not an office, but a manifestation of the Holy Spirit's presence to guide the church. In total, the Greek root ποιμην is used forty times in the NT. The most relevant uses of the Greek word ποιμήν are in the following eighteen examples.

- 11 times ποιμήν is used in Matthew, Mark, and John predominantly as an analogy; as shepherd is to flock so God is to Israel.

- 4 times ποιμήν is used in Luke in reference to the shepherds who came to see the birth of Jesus.

- 2 times in Hebrews and Peter in reference to Jesus as the Shepherd of God's covenant people (the church).

- 1 time in Ephesians in reference to a gift from God's Spirit used to establish the church and help her grow in maturity.

The Greek ποιμήν is most often translated "shepherd," but is also the same word for "pastor." Pastoring is a gift given to the church to help guide the young in faith. Those who hold the office of elder are given the Spirit-gifting to pastor. The term "pastor" in the New Testament is not an office; any more than is apostle, prophet, teacher or evangelist, it is a gifting from God. As Hoehner observes, "Scripture consistently maintains a distinction between the office and the gift. Eldership is an office, whereas pastor-teacher is a gift."[1] Therefore, it is fair to make the following conclusions:

---

1. Hoehner, "Can a Woman," 763.

- Elders are gifted by the Spirit to pastor God's people.

- Elders are gifted by the Spirit to teach God's people.

"Pastoring" and "teaching" are just two of these give unique giftings given to the elders so that they can effectively guide, protect, and grow God's people into unity of faith. Nowhere in the New Testament is the word ποιμήν used as a title for leaders in the church and this understanding has shaped my own practice.

When I planted my first church many years ago, people would come into our fellowship and say to me, "Hello Pastor Joe," and I would usually reply, "Hi, it is great to meet you, but please feel free to call me Joe."

Why was this my response? Because I wanted people to know that my title was not "pastor." I did not want a title to become a barrier to our true relationship as brothers and sisters in Christ. I did not want my Spirit-gifting of "shepherd" to be reduced to an honorary title of man-made tradition; because shepherding God's people is so much more important than being called a pastor.

So regardless if one prefers to use the term "pastor" or "shepherd" . . . the real question remains, what is a ποιμήν?

- "Pastor" is *not* a title of leadership.

- "Pastor" is *not* the name of church-office.

- "Pastor" is *not* about wielding power over others.

- "Pastor" is *not* a synonym for "elder."

But:

- "Pastor" *is* one of five foundational giftings given by the Holy Spirit to help build church.

- The gift of "pastoring" *is* given to some big brothers and sisters so they can guide their younger siblings into maturity.

- The gift of "pastoring" *is* given to some elders so they can model servanthood to the flock.

So if "pastor" is a gifting and not an office, this raises the question, of women in leadership. Should women be "pastors" in the church?

Women and the Pastoral Gift

Whenever this topic is addressed, the various responses fall into two camps:

"I value women as pastors in the church, and therefore I have a low view of the Bible."

Or:

"I value the Bible, therefore I will never accept women as pastors in the church."

Let me say clearly that I believe both of these views are in error! The good news is that there is an alternative to the above. The answer is not going back in time to the "good old days." This is well stated by Nancy Leigh DeMos and Mary A. Kassian in their book, *True Woman 101*.

> The solution isn't to try to rewind the clock to the 1950s, and squeeze women back into that culture's "Leave It to Beaver" stereotype. No. The solution—the biblical solution—is to embrace the Word of God, and ask Him to help us figure out how to live out His divine design in this culture.[2]

I believe in the authority of the Bible and trust it as the source for my doctrine, ethics, and ministry practice *and because* of my love for the Scripture, I believe the church needs to recognize that some women are gifted by the Holy Spirit as pastors.[3]

Okay, but what does that mean for women to be a pastor?

Am I suggesting that we need more mega-church, superstar paparazzi women pastors like we have men pastors? No, I am not arguing for the status quo. I am arguing for a biblical order to the

---

2. DeMoss and Kassian, *True Woman 101*, Kindle loc. 2911–13.

3. Sumner, *Men and Women in the Church*, 216.

church, and to do this I must work hard to faithfully apply the Scripture:

- Where the Bible speaks clearly, I need to speak clearly.
- Where the Bible is silent, I need to be silent.
- And in all cases I need to speak and act with charity.

If then I am faithful to the Word, I must accept that some women can be gifted by the Spirit as pastors (shepherds) in the church. But, I am going to apply that truth in a way you may not expect. To do that, I need to clarify what it means to be a pastor.

As I stated previously, the Greek word ποιμήν is used only one time in the NT in reference to a gift from God's Spirit (Eph 4:11) and nowhere does it say this gifting is only for men, or only for the elders, but we do see examples in the New Testament of where women are given the charge to shepherd (pastor) and teach well the doctrines of the faith (Titus 2:3–4).

The problem we have in the church today in the West is that too much of our ministry practice is based on guesswork about what the word "pastor" means. The guessing needs to stop. We need to cut out the false expectations put on women by Western culture, and discard what is a fundamentally flawed view of ministry. In the previous section, I offered four insights into what "a pastor is *not*," so here let me expand on each of these four as they relate to women in pastoral leadership.

Unload Cultural Expectations

When it comes to the role of pastor, the church has made too many decisions based on culture and not enough from Scripture. We have built a system of "pastor as CEO" that is not in the Bible and then forced that system onto the Scripture. Until this problem is corrected, we will never accept women into their proper—God-ordained—place both inside and outside the church.

"Pastor" is not a title of leadership

This is true for both men and women. If we follow the biblical usage of ποιμήν, neither sex should hold onto the "title" of pastor. This does not mean we should reject biblical authority and leadership, it just means that biblical authority is deeper than the titles we have created for ourselves.

"Pastor" is not the name of church office

Over the years, I have had many women friends point out that because they cannot hold the "office" of pastor, they cannot get the Government benefits of the housing allowance, tax deductions, and other societal benefits. However, when we recognize the biblical distinction between the office of elder and the gift of pastoring, this barrier is easily removed.

There is therefore no biblical barrier to women who dedicate themselves to full-time ministry being able to get these benefits.[4] Tax breaks and denominational ordination are not what it means to be a pastor in the church. These are cultural conventions and should be made available to anyone, man or woman, who is approved by their local church or denomination to teach and preach the gospel.

"Pastor" is not a synonym for "elder"

Elders in the church are given the task of shepherding the flock in a unique way that keeps the church ready for the return of the Chief Shepherd who is Christ (John 10:16).

The ministry of elders to shepherd and oversee is not the same as the Spirit ordained gift of shepherding. As mentioned previously, Eph 4:11 tells us that "pastor" *is* one of five foundational gifts given by the Holy Spirit to help build church. This gift *is* given

---

4. Boehner makes this same conclusion in his article "Can a Woman," 771. And while I do not share fully in his analysis and conclusion, his overall point is persuasive.

to some mature brothers and sisters in the church so that they can guide their younger siblings into maturity.

Older women are to pastor the younger women and older men are to pastor the younger men (Titus 2:1–5). Before going any further, I find it necessary to address the issue of discipleship. Many will read this statement that women should shepherd women as way of diminishing the role of women in leadership. This is a deeply saddening statement that reflects the dysfunction of leadership structures in the church. What we fail to see from our modern perspective is the biblical value God places on the elder women leading the younger women and the elder men leading the younger men. This kind of generational faith is what God values above all else. Susan Hunt makes this very same point.

> In recent years I have observed a troubling phenomenon. Many women of my generation have relinquished this high calling of nurturing younger women. Everywhere I go I meet young women who long for spiritual mothers.
>
> My generation has abandoned this calling for many reasons. Some think they have nothing to offer. Some are intimidated by the intelligence and giftedness of the younger women. And some have decided this is the season to indulge themselves.
>
> I plead with you not to squander this season of your lives. You have a perspective on life to share. Your sensibilities have been tempered by time. Your faith has been stretched and strengthened by your life-experiences.
>
> I plead with the Church to equip women for this ministry. God is gifting His Church with incredible young women. They are a sacred trust; we must be good stewards. Many of them are first-generation Christians. Many are separated from their families because of the mobility of our society. We must teach them the truths of biblical womanhood. We must teach them how to pass on the faith to the next generation. The consequences of our accepting or abandoning this calling will reverberate through several generations.[5]

---

5. Hunt, "Seasons of a Woman's Life," 9.

So turning our minds back to the main passage in Titus 2:1–5, it does not say that all older women are given the Spirit-gifting of "pastoring," but since it does make clear that women are shepherds, it is not unreasonable, nor a violation of explicit apostolic teaching, to conclude that some of these women will be especially gifted by the Spirit as pastors to help equip the church to grow in holiness.

The gift of "pastor" is not the same as the office of elder. So while all elders are gifted as pastors, not all pastors (men or women) are called to the office of elder. Some men may pastor the church without holding the office of elder. Some women may pastor in the church without holding the office of elder. This is true for any of the five foundational giftings given to the church.

The gift of "teacher" is not the same as the office of elder. So while all elders are gifted to teach, not all teachers (men or women) are called to the office of elder. Some men may teach or preach to the church without holding the office of elder. Some women may teach or preach to the church without holding the office of elder.

A Right View of Ministry

Our culture is obsessed with power . . . the church is obsessed with power . . . but the Bible is not!

"Pastor" is *not* about wielding power over others.

One argument I often hear is that women need to be pastors so they can "share the power/authority"[6] with men. The problem here is that pastoral ministry is not about wielding power—at least not from a biblical perspective. In practice, unfortunately, the typical pastor has chosen to imitate the world and set himself up as the "man with power" and in seeking equality women have fought to get a share of that power, but this is not God's design for biblical leadership. Take, for example, this cartoon I created many years ago while living in Washington state.[7]

6. Beach, "Women in Church Leadership."
7. Miller, "Blind Foxes & Velvet Fences."

This cartoon comes from a true story of a local pastor who, after each service, sits behind a velvet rope and allows the people to come through a line to shake his hand. The people are also allowed to give him money as they pass through the line. I look at this image as a metaphor for ministry in general, and specifically how we have turned "pastor" into "power." This is not what women (or men for that matter) should aspire to. This is not the kind of power that needs to be shared. This is the kind of power that needs to be rejected by the church.

So when I say women should be pastors,

- I am not saying women need to "share" the power.
- I am not saying women need to be "empowered."

We are not the world. It is striking to note that "feminism is about women's power. Christianity is about Christ's power."[8] Contrary to the ways of our world, any man or woman who wants to be a pastor must be about "dis-empowerment" . . . that is giving up power so that they can serve, sacrifice and love the church. Jesus is our example, as the head pastor he gave up all his power and laid down his life for his flock. Paul's letter to the church in Philippi makes this very point to the early church who struggled with the same issues facing us today.

> Do nothing from selfish ambition or conceit, but in humility count others more significant than yourselves. Let each of you look not only to his own interests, but also to the interests of others. Have this mind among yourselves, which is yours in Christ Jesus, who, though he was in the form of God, did not count equality with God a thing to be grasped, but emptied himself, by taking the form of a servant, being born in the likeness of men. And being found in human form, he humbled himself by becoming obedient to the point of death, even death on a cross. (Phil 2:3–8 ESV)

Same Spirit-Gifting; Unique People

The same hermeneutic that leads me to conclude only men are elders, leads me to conclude that some women are gifted by the Spirit as pastors in the church. However, this does not mean we need to accept the world's view that men and women are the same . . . they are not. Both men and women are created in the image of God and *both* are needed to reflect the fullness of his glory. The reason God created men and women, is because each sex has unique qualities

8. Sumner, *Men and Women in the Church*, 33.

43

that are necessary to be the church. So while women and men can both have a pastoral gifting, that does not mean they both function the same way in the church.

Acknowledging the high call God has placed on women to help lead in the church, does not mean we have to blur the distinctive beauty between the sexes. Nor does this uniqueness allow us, the church, to marginalize women and minimize their value as leaders in the family of God—which has all too frequently been the case. Men and women are unique and will fulfill the role of "pastor" in their own unique way. Kassian and DeMoss express the need for diversity this way.

> The Bible presents a design for True Womanhood that applies to all women—at any age and at any stage of life—old, young; single, married, divorced, widowed; with children or without, whatever. Its design applies to women of every personality type, every educational level, every career track, every socioeconomic status, and every culture. God's design transcends social customs, time, and circumstance.[9]

Living out God's design for women in leadership means we should not force women to lead like men, especially men who have abused their role as leaders. especially men who have abused their role as leaders. Women need to lead beyond the cultural expectation and lead in the light of the eternal light of Christ. We must decide to value women in the church and be intentional in honoring their giftedness. Once again as Kassian and DeMoss remind us,

> That's not to say that our decisions don't matter. In His Word God has given us timeless principles about womanhood that transcend culture. It's important that we wrestle with how to implement these principles. We need to rely on the Holy Spirit's guidance to help us figure out how to apply them in our particular situation. But we must avoid a cookie-cutter mentality. We are all unique. Every woman's circumstances are distinct. We each need to carefully discern how to apply God's principles in our

9. DeMoss and Kassian, *True Woman 101*, Kindle loc. 245–48.

own lives, and we can encourage one another in that process; but it's not up to us to determine how they must be applied in other women's lives.[10]

In summary, in the New Testament, elder describes an office a few select men occupy and apostle, prophet, pastor, teacher and evangelist describes a variety of giftings from the Holy Spirit shared by many chosen men and women.[11]

Elders and a Diversity of Giftings

There are a variety of giftings given by the Holy Spirit to equip elders. All elders teach, all elders pastor, but within the team of leaders there is a functional diversity that reflects the overall design of God's family. My fellow church planter Peyton Jones describes well the diversity by design within the elder team. He writes,

> Have you ever wondered why there are plural "elders" in the New Testament church? In the West the elders are either toadies to the CEO pastor who hope for preaching scraps to fall from the table, or they are there to make sure that the pastor doesn't get a big head, steal money, or sleep with your wife. What if the elders of the church were the apostle, prophet, evangelist, shepherd, and teacher? What if the multiplicity of elders in the first-century churches existed because these five roles were essential to modeling the full ministry of Jesus? Together they would keep the church in a correct nutritional balance. Each leader with a unique emphasis would create a healthy tension in the leadership team between five separate areas.[12]

Not every elder is gifted for the same thing. One practical area of application is preaching. All elders will teach the gospel, but preaching is only one small aspect of that calling. I am a strong

10. Ibid., Kindle loc. 3994–99.

11. Summer, *Men and Women in the Church*, 215.

12. Jones, *Church Zero*, 125. See also Newton and Schmucker, "Elders in the Life of the Church," 35.

believer in building preaching teams so that the church can hear many diverse voices sharing the one message of Christ. Not every elder may be on the preaching team and this also means that people who are not elders, but gifted to preach, can be incorporated into that team.[13] I recognize that this idea seems radical to many pastors who have been trained to believe that there should only be one primary communicator in each church. Over the years of promoting teaching teams to my students, this is one concept that causes the most confusion since they have simply not observed preaching teams in action.[14] But, building these teams is important for several reasons.

First, the "one-man preacher" approach is one of the very reasons so many pastors feel alone in ministry because they have no one to share the load of preaching. If we hope to preserve our leaders from succumbing to the Monday morning blues, then we need to surround them with a team of gifted preachers who can share the load.

Second, the church must do better in developing the next generation of preachers. Giving young men and women the opportunity to exercise their Spirit-gifting under the supervision of the elders and amid the loving arms of their church family is the best way to build for the future. The purpose of every gifting is to build up and disciple, so every man or woman gifted to preach must find a way to build up the next generation of preachers.

Third, when we approach preaching as a team sport, we grow our congregations—not around the personality of one man—but around the very Scripture which is the source of our one shared message. When the people hear the one gospel from a variety of speakers; each with their own background, experience, and cultural perspective, the church grows with a better formed view of the absolute truth of the Bible (2 Tim 2:2).

The most significant aspect in discussing the diversity of giftings among the elder team is that the office of elder is a reflection of

---

13. Newton and Schmucker, "Elders in the Life of the Church," 176.

14. See my video series for more information, "Video Training."

the infinite nature of God who builds a church where each one of us is dependent upon the other to manifest his goodness and holiness.

Now moving beyond gifting, let's look more deeply at exactly what it means when we say that eldership is an "office" of the church.

Elder Is More Than an Office

The problem with using the term "office" is that it comes with a lot of baggage. In church history, some have argued for a five-fold office[15] to lead the church, while others have argued for a three-fold office.[16] In the New Testament, there really are only two recognized offices: elder and deacon. Yes, "elder" is an office of leadership in the church (1 Tim 3:1), but the elder's purpose is not to simply occupy a position of leadership; it is both an office and a function.[17]

- The elder's authority does not come from an office, but from Jesus Christ.

- The elder is not called to serve an office, he is called to serve the church.

Eldership, while affirmed by the church and her elders, is primarily a manifestation of the Holy Spirit's power and presence among the church. We must never cease to value the Spirit-ordained leadership of the elder.

> Until I come, devote yourself to the public reading of Scripture, to exhortation, to teaching. Do not neglect the gift you have, which was given you by prophecy when the council of elders laid their hands on you. Practice these

15. Edward Irving in the late 18th and early 19th centuries provides one example of how the fivefold office was popularized in Europe and America. See my book *Promise of the Father*, 28–32.

16. In the sixteenth-century Anabaptist tradition, "the polity was congregational as was that of many Anabaptist churches on the Continent. It called, however, for a threefold ministry of pastor, deacon, and elder, again indicating possible Calvinistic influence." Estep, *Anabaptist Story*, 280.

17. Mappes, "New Testament Elder," 85.

things, immerse yourself in them, so that all may see your progress. Keep a close watch on yourself and on the teaching. Persist in this, for by so doing you will save both yourself and your hearers. (1 Tim 4:13–16 ESV)

The New Testament makes it clear, every believer is given some gifting from the Spirit for service to the body and this includes the elder. The most unique aspect of eldership in the New Covenant, is that eldership in the church is less about "office," and more about a special calling from the Holy Spirit. Read what Paul has to say here in ch. 12 of his letter to the Corinthians as they struggled to understand the nature of Spirit-gifting.

Now there are varieties of gifts, but the same Spirit; and there are *varieties of service*, but the *same Lord*; and there are *varieties of activities*, but it is the *same God* who empowers them all in everyone. *To each* is given the manifestation of the Spirit for the *common good*. For to one is given through the Spirit the utterance of wisdom, and to another the utterance of knowledge according to the *same Spirit*, to another faith by the *same Spirit*, to another gifts of healing by the *one Spirit*, to another the working of miracles, to another prophecy, to another the ability to distinguish between spirits, to another various kinds of tongues, to another the interpretation of tongues. *All these are empowered by one and the same Spirit, who apportions to each one individually as he wills.* For just as the body is one and has many members, and all the members of the body, though many, are one body, so it is with Christ. For in one Spirit we were all baptized into one body—Jews or Greeks, slaves or free—and all were made to drink of one Spirit. For the body does not consist of one member but of many. If the foot should say, "Because I am not a hand, I do not belong to the body," that would not make it any less a part of the body. And if the ear should say, "Because I am not an eye, I do not belong to the body," that would not make it any less a part of the body. If the whole body were an eye, where would be the sense of hearing? If the whole body were an ear, where would be the sense of smell? But as it is, *God arranged the members in the body, each one of them, as he chose. If all were a single member, where would the body be?* As it is, there are many parts, yet one body. The eye cannot say to the hand, "I have no need of you," nor again the head to the feet, "I have no need of you." *On the contrary, the parts of the body that seem to be weaker are indispensable, and on those parts of the body that we think less honorable we bestow the greater honor, and our un-presentable parts are treated with greater modesty, which our more presentable parts do not require.* But God has so composed the body, giving greater honor to the part that lacked it, that there may be no division in the body, but that the members may have the same care for one another. If one member suffers, all suffer together; if one member is honored, all rejoice together. Now you are the body of Christ and individually members of it. And God has appointed in the church first apostles, second proph-ets, third teachers, then miracles, then gifts of healing, helping, administrating, and various kinds of tongues. Are all apostles? Are all prophets? *Are all teachers?* Do all work miracles? Do all possess gifts of healing? Do all speak with tongues? Do all interpret? *But earnestly desire the higher gifts. And I will show you a still more excellent way.* (1 Cor 12:4–31 ESV, emphasis added)

Every member of God's family has something to offer, but not everyone can offer the same thing. Paul is very clear, everyone in the body offers a unique manifestation of the Spirit for the com-mon good. In his study of 1 Corinthians 12, Jackson makes this bold observation:

Wherever the Spirit of God is breathing new life into the church, the priesthood of believers is being rediscovered. So, too, is the spiritual giftedness of that priesthood, because a heightened awareness of either of these leads inevitably to the others.[18]

These unique giftings are the source of strength and power for unity in the body. If everyone tries to be an eye, the body will fail. If everyone tries to be an apostle, the body will fail. This same

18. Jackson, "Concerning Spiritual Gifts," 59.

principle of diverse manifestations for the glory of God applies to the office of elder. If everyone tries to be an elder, the body will fail; but if nobody serves as an elder the body will fail. The body needs healthy elders.

> I therefore, a prisoner for the Lord, urge you to walk in a manner worthy of the calling to which you have been called, with all humility and gentleness, with patience, bearing with one another in love, *eager to maintain the unity of the Spirit in the bond of peace.* There is one body and one Spirit—just as you were called to the one hope that belongs to your call—one Lord, one faith, one baptism, one God and Father of all, who is over all and through all and in all. But *grace was given to each one of us according to the measure of Christ's gift.* . . . And he gave the apostles, the prophets, the evangelists, the *shepherds* and teachers, to equip the saints for the work of ministry, for building up the body of Christ, until we all attain to the unity of the faith and of the knowledge of the Son of God, to mature manhood, to the measure of the stature of the fullness of Christ, so that we may no longer be children, tossed to and fro by the waves and carried about by every wind of doctrine, by human cunning, by craftiness in deceitful schemes. (Eph 4:1–14 ESV, emphasis added)

While recognizing the unique call of "eldership" to serve the local church, we must never forget that Spirit-led elders are not given as a replacement for the Spirit-gifted ministry of body—they are part of it! Only a few men are called to the task of eldership, but every member of the body is called and gifted for a great purpose. Hayes states this well:

> All believers are to be engaged in the ministry of the church. "Everyone," wrote Augustine, "is the servant of Christ in the same way Christ is also a servant." While the term "calling" can be used in the popular sense of the work of men and women in ministry, "it can be used in exactly the same sense of a salesman, a lawyer, a teacher or an actor." In other words ministry is neither an option for believers nor a special class of believers.

In the New Testament all believers are called of God. Yet some believers because of their spiritual gifts may be separated for a full-time exercise of ministry. However, this dedication, or even ordination, does not give special privileges to these individuals as special channels of grace nor does it elevate ministers above those who are in so-called "secular" callings.[19]

With a clear understanding of elders as uniquely Spirit-ordained members of the body, and the importance of every member using their gifting to grow the family, our next chapter will look at how these men are selected for eldership.

19. Hayes, "Call to Ministry," 97.

5

Character Still Counts

SITTING IN THE MIDST of all these young Seattle church planters, I could not understand what they saw in the man leading the
conference. The fast-growing mega-church hosting the conference
was known for its plurality of elders, and I wanted to learn from
them. But with every anecdote that Mike told, I started to question my decision to associate with this group. The guy on stage
seemed just as power-hungry as any other solo-pastor I had ever
met . . . and he was celebrated for it. These young leaders liked the
stories Mike told; each one demonstrating just how powerful he
was and how much he controlled the men "under his command"
(his words, not mine).

After the session ended I asked one of the guys near me for
his take on Mike as a leader. He said, "Sure, Mike is a little ar-
rogant, but he knows it. But look at what he has built here. This is
just who he is." And with a metaphorical nod and a wink, he let me
know that if I wanted to be in Mike's tribe, I would learn to accept
the "boyish charm" of this successful leader.

As I looked over the paperwork the group handed out that
described the moral qualities of an elder, I could not help but notice that Mike would never qualify. He was the leader of the frat
house and so the rules did not apply to him, but if a common man
like me wanted to join . . . I was expected to be a humble follower
of Mike's leadership and submit to his authority.

Years later, Mike's arrogance would be his downfall. As his abusive leadership impacted more and more people, Mike refused accountability, he restructured the leadership to consolidate power, he created tiers of eldership (regular elders, executive elders and the lead elder), he rejected the discipline of the other elders, and he was ultimately forced to resigned in disgrace. In the end, his mega-church ceased to exist without Mike at the nexus of control.

The church does not need any more leaders like Mike who claim the name "elder," but refuse to live up to the qualities described in the Scripture. So what does it take to be an elder and how should we select the men who will lead? The New Testament gives some very clear direction.

Choose Elders Wisely

An elder is given to the church by the Holy Spirit to shepherd the flock, but the selection of an elder goes beyond giftedness and calling. The doctrinal purity, character, reputation, family life, abilities, and passions of an elder are also vital to his leadership of the church.

This of course brings up the question, "who does the 'appointing'?" How are elders chosen, selected, elected and/or ordained? Confusion has persisted over time in many churches; are elders given authority and power by the congregation or is their appointment and authority from God alone?[1] The New Testament does not give an exact process so we are faced to dig a little deeper into the language used by the inspired authors.

Outside of the two uses related to appointing either elders or deacons, the word "appoint" (καθίστημι) is used twenty-one times in the New Testament. Some of the unique uses include the following examples:

- In Rom 5:19, all mankind was appointed (made) sinners by the actions of Adam and appointed (made) righteous by the cross of Christ.

- In Heb 8:3, we find that priests were appointed by the law.

1. Hodge, "Review of Theories," 186.

- In Jas 4:4, we are told that anyone who choses friendship with the world appoints himself as an enemy of God.

- In 2 Pet 1:8, we are told that our increasing virtue will appoint us to effective and fruitful knowledge of Christ.

From these select examples, we can discern a very diverse meaning of the Greek word καθίστημι. This diversity of meaning, does not necessarily make the process of understanding "appointment" easier, but it does illustrate the hermeneutical dilemma . . . how should we appoint our elders? To get closer to our goal, let's move on then from a study of the Greek, to the context for how this word is used in the most relevant passages.

Paul instructed Titus (already an elder "appointed" by Paul) to "appoint" more elders in the church according to the instructions he had already given (Titus 1:5). But what were those exact instructions? Did Titus alone "appoint" the new elders? Were all the elders involved? Was the congregation included in this process? We don't fully know.

We can gain some insight to the process from the example of how deacons were "appointed" by the apostles in Acts 6. In this case, they were "appointed" (καθίστημι) by the apostolic laying on of hands, but only after they were "selected" (ἐπισκέπτομαι) by the church. Additionally, in Acts 13, Paul and Barnabas are "set apart" (ἀφορίζω) by the Holy Spirit and affirmed to their mission by the church with the laying on of hands. Later in their first missionary journey, they appointed elders in each church. And what can we discern from the instructions given in 1 Tim 5:22 to impartially restore an elder through laying on of hands (1 Tim 5:22)? What role, if any, does the congregation play in this process?

The conclusion one makes on how to "appoint" elders will, in large part, depend on church tradition and the hermeneutic used for interpreting the word "appoint" (καθίστημι) found in the key passages mentioned above.[2] Some will conclude that καθίστημι excludes the congregation completely from the process

2. Acts 6:3 and Titus 1:5.

of appointment.[3] Others will conclude that καθίστημι demands the inclusion of the congregation in the appointment of elders.[4]

In looking at each of these cases, I think it is fair to conclude that the inability to come to a consensus on the exact process of "appointing" elders[5] means that God has left to each local congregation some discretion.[6] Regardless of how each church chooses to appoint elders, there are some good guidelines for all who are involved.

- The one who aspires to lead must first and foremost, called by the Holy Spirit.

- A future elder must be observed by the congregation over a period of time to have demonstrated the qualities necessary to lead.

- A future elder must be appointed by the existing elders who have clear direction from the Spirit and affirmation from the congregation.

There is certainly room within this to accommodate a variety of traditions, but one thing is clear: elders who were not well chosen became divisive to the church. In Paul's first letter to Timothy, we see how some elders in Ephesus were teaching a corrupt gospel (1 Tim 1:3–4). Consequently, Paul warned Timothy to make sure that the selection of all elders was done with caution.

> Do not admit a charge against an elder except on the evidence of two or three witnesses. As for those who persist in sin, rebuke them in the presence of all, so that the rest may stand in fear. In the presence of God and of Christ Jesus and of the elect angels I charge you to keep these rules without prejudging, doing nothing from partiality. Do not be hasty in the laying on of hands, nor take part in the sins of others; keep yourself pure. (1 Tim 5:19–22 ESV)

---

3. Park, "Review of Suggested Modifications," 392–93.

4. Newton and Schmucker, "Elders in the Life of the Church," 68.

5. Gray, *Biblical Encyclopedia and Museum*, 136.

6. Newton and Schmucker, "Elders in the Life of the Church," 68.

Elders in the church had a significant leadership role in keeping the church doctrinally pure, and so their public appointment by the laying on of hands should not to be taken lightly.[7]

The Qualities of an Elder

The great teacher, Paul, gives excellent instruction to both Timothy and Titus on how to recognize the men whom the Spirit has called to serve as elders among the church.[8] It is interesting to note that unlike the Jewish system that emphasized age as a requirement,[9] the elder in the New Covenant was established by maturity in faith.

Select Elders Based on Doctrine and Character

As you read through the Pastoral Epistles, there is a clear rhetorical cohesion between doctrine and character. If an elder has a corrupt theology, his character will be corrupt. If an elder teaches sound doctrine, a sound character will follow.[10]

Select Elders Based on Character

1. "Temperate"—a man who demonstrates a balanced emotional life and avoids the extremes.

7. "A logical connection between v. 21 and v. 22 is readily available. In light of the solemn necessity of rebuking sinning Elders, candidates for such a position must be chosen carefully . . . a call to purity makes perfect sense after a warning not to share in the sins of another. One is the positive restatement of the other." See Van Neste, *Cohesion and Structure*, 65.

8. 1 Tim 3:1–7; Titus 1:1–9; see also 1 Pet 5:1–4.

9. Luke 3:23.

10. I developed the following lists over many years and pulled them from multiple sources. Long before I ever considered using them in a book, I used them to train others. Now I find that I cannot cite any one source for these lists, but I know I relied on the wisdom of others to make them. Thanks to all who contributed to this list, and my apologies if I have not given the proper attribution.

2. "Prudent"—a man who shows good judgment, common sense and not given to frivolous activities.

3. "Not Addicted to Wine"—an elder should not be addicted to alcoholic drink, but just as important he should not demonstrate an addictive personality.

4. "Not Pugnacious"—not given to physical violence, brawling, or abusive speech and he avoids silly arguments that lead to fights or division in the body.

5. "Gentle"—a man who demonstrates patience, forgives easily, and is considerate to everyone.

6. "Not Quarrelsome"—a man who will defend the gospel, defend the flock, refrain from theological speculation (1 Tim 1:3–4), and do so in a peaceable manner.

7. "Not Greedy"—an elder must be free from love of money, not allowing money to distort his mission to the church, or seek eldership for personal gain or financial profit.

8. "Not Young in Faith"—a man who serves as elder must not be a new believer, but rather one that has been saved long enough to have developed and demonstrated a maturity of wisdom suitable for leading the church. Notice Paul's example from his first missionary journey where he did not appoint elders among the newly formed churches for close to two years in some cases (Acts 14:21–23).

9. "Not Self-Willed"—an elder puts the needs of others above his own, does not try and get his way, and demonstrates humility in his service.

10. "Not Quick-Tempered"—anger is not always a sin, but a man who does not allow anger to come quickly, even when hurt or wronged by another, will make a good elder.

11. "Loves What Is Good"—an elder is not only loyal to moral and ethical values, he takes pleasure in doing good deeds.

12. "Just"—a man whose decisions are fair and honest and who sacrifices his rights and his needs for the good of others.

13. "Devout"—an elder is devoted to God in worship, refuses to compromise the gospel, and does not give in to social or political pressures.

14. "Self-Controlled"—able to control himself under adverse or tempting circumstances, as well as demonstrate constraint in the physical pleasures of life.

Select Elders Based on Reputation

1. "Above Reproach"—a man who has no questionable conduct that would bring accusations against himself or against the church.

2. "Hospitable"—a man who demonstrates a personal warmth and strong affection for all people.

3. "Good Reputation with Those Outside the Church"—notwithstanding those who would persecute the church, an elder must have an ethically upright testimony, demonstrate peace, and shows love toward the lost.

4. "An Example to the Flock"—even through his imperfections, an elder must be the spiritual big brother and lead by his voice and by his example.

Select Elders Based on Family Life

1. "Husband of One Wife"—literally an elder is "a one-woman man."[11] If single, an elder is not flirtatious and lives a sexually pure lifestyle. If married, he demonstrates total satisfaction with, and affection for, his wife.

---

11. Glasscock offers an excellent discussion of the different interpretations of this passage related to diverse and elder qualifications. See Glasscock, "Husband of One Wife," 187–99.

2. "Manages His Own Household Well"—an elder demonstrates spiritual leadership of his family and does not allow his personal affairs or finances to get out of control. If an elder cannot manage his own household, he cannot manage the household of God.

3. "Children under Control with Dignity"—if an elder has been given children, they should demonstrate obedience and respect. He must not be harsh or brutal with his children so as to cause them to rebel. He must be a man who leads through loving discipline, gives consistent training and biblical correction.

Select Elders based on Giftings and Abilities

1. "Able to Teach and Be Taught"—an elder need not have any formal education, but he must be able to read, understand, disciple, teach and preach the Scripture. He must demonstrate that he has the gift of teaching, is being led by the Spirit, and is open to being taught by others.

2. "Holding Fast the Word of Truth"—a man who holds firm to the doctrines of the apostles and does not compromise the Scripture with false tradition or denominationalism.

3. "Exhort with Sound Doctrine"—a man who encourages others with his teaching and does not place guilt or works on the family.

4. "Refute Those Who Contradict"—an elder must stand against and stop false teaching that would harm the flock or distort the gospel.

Select Elders Based on Passion

1. "Not Compelled to Serve"—a man who serves as elder must do so with a passion to serve and not be forced into leadership by others. An elder must lead from a pure motive, a clear gifting from the Spirit, and a recognized calling rather than a desire for reputation or prominence.

Eldership Is a Lifestyle

Wayne Grudem makes some interesting observations about these lists and how they should be applied in our churches.

> When Paul lists the qualifications for elders, it is significant that he combines requirements concerning character traits and heart attitudes with requirements that cannot be fulfilled in a short time but will only become evident over a period of several years of faithful Christian living. . . . Those who are choosing elders in churches today would do well to look carefully at candidates in the light of these qualifications, and to look for these character traits and patterns of godly living rather than worldly achievement, fame, or success.[12]

This observation takes on special meaning in a culture that is consumed by celebrity pastors.

Several years ago I was working a booth at a conference in Los Angeles, California, for a popular Christian pastor.[13] A man, let's call him Tim, came to my table and noticed a book written by another famous pastor. Tim turned to the stranger next to him, pointed toward the book, and with great pride exclaimed, "That's my pastor."

The man either did not hear Tim, or he decided to ignore him; so this time Tim picked up the book and said, "That man is my pastor."

12. Grudem, *Systematic Theology*, 918.
13. This story was adapted from my post "Paparazzi Pastors."

The other guy walked off—Tim was clearly hoping the man would be more impressed.

Tim turned to me, a captive audience at the booth, and proclaimed, "That man is my pastor."

Tim's "pastor" lead a popular church in Seattle and since I had recently moved from that area, I was interested to know if we had some friends in common, so I asked, "Oh, so you are from Seattle? What brings you to LA?"

Tim's answer surprised me: "No," he said, "I live here in LA."

Now I was intrigued. How could Pastor John, be Tim's pastor if he lived 1,200 miles away? So I asked, "Did you recently move here from Seattle?"

"No," Tim replied, "my church meets in my house and we watch Pastor John's sermon every week on DVD."

I immediately felt a twinge of sorrow—sorrow for Tim and sorrow for the church and what she had become. Pastor John may be an engaging Bible teacher, but he certainly has not taught his followers a biblical definition of what it means to be an elder who shepherds God's people.

Read the Pastoral Epistles from the Apostle Paul, an elder is a not a talking head who "phones it in" via DVD. An elder is someone with a gifting from the Holy Spirit to be a shepherd, a caretaker, a guardian, a servant, and a lover of God's people.

It is impossible for a anyone to be "my pastor" via DVD or multisite video. He may inspire, educate, or even motivate, but he is not fulfilling the biblical role of elder in my life or yours. Sadly, it did not matter to Tim that Pastor John wasn't really living out the biblical role of "my pastor." Rather, what mattered most to Tim was that he had a claim to fame through his paparazzi pastor.

But popularity is not what makes one qualified to be an elder in God's family. Successfully marketing our sermons and books, regardless of how good the content, does not make someone a spiritual leader. Worldly success is not the standard for choosing our elders, as Grudem writes,

> Especially in churches in western industrial societies, there seems to be a tendency to think that success in the

world of business (or law, or medicine, or government) is an indication of suitability for the office of elder, but this is not the teaching of the New Testament. It reminds us that elders are to be "examples to the flock" in their daily lives, and that would certainly include their own personal relationships with God in Bible reading, prayer, and worship.[14]

Did you catch what he is saying? Business success is not the same as biblical success. The two are not mutually exclusive, but we need to make sure our elders model the later before they are recognized as leaders in the church.

Richard Baxter offers a salient comment on this very topic. The terminology he uses is a bit different than what I am using in this book, but I think the following sentiment is a good summary to what we need in our elders.

> The ministerial work must be carried on purely for God and the salvation of souls, not for any private ends of our own. A wrong end makes all the work bad as from us, how good whatsoever it may be in its own nature. It is not serving God, but ourselves, if we do it not for God, but for ourselves. They who engage in this as a common work, to make a trade of it for their worldly livelihood, will find that they have chosen a bad trade, though a good employment. Self–denial is of absolute necessity in every Christian, but it is doubly necessary in a minister, as without it he cannot do God an hour's faithful service. Hard studies, much knowledge, and excellent preaching, if the ends be not right, is but more glorious hypocritical sinning. The saying of Bernard is commonly known:
>
> Some desire to know merely for the sake of knowing, and that is shameful curiosity. Some desire to know that they may sell their knowledge, and that too is shameful. Some desire to know for reputation's sake, and that is shameful vanity. But there are some who desire to know that they may edify others, and that is praiseworthy; and there are some who desire to know that they themselves may be edified, and that is wise.[15]

14. Grudem, *Systematic Theology*, 918.

15. Baxter, *Reformed Pastor*, 111.

Down but Not Destroyed

As you review each of the qualities from this chapter, keep something in mind . . . in a shared-leadership model with a plurality of elders, it is much easier to handle situations where the elder falls short.

We all have struggles. Every one of us has times when the pressures of life demand we take a break, recharge and get right with God. Every elder will face trials that necessitate a time to step-down and recalibrate. This is not a defeat. Stepping down does not mean we have to live in defeat. This is not a call to "quit" the ministry. It is our human condition which means there are seasons when good leaders need to rest. This is where a plurality of elders has great advantage over the pastor CEO model.

With a single "senior pastor," there is far more pressure to hide flaws in character. Your job is on the line. Weakness can mean a loss of power and influence. When issues do eventually come to the surface—and they always do—churches can find it difficult to offer godly correction to the senior pastor who is then feels forced to leave the church. This can eventually destroy a man and, at the same time, leave the church wounded.

In contrast to the senior pastor, with a team of elders working together, any one elder who needs time away to work on any of the aforementioned godly qualities, can do so without fear of the church falling apart. The other elders can both keep their struggling brother accountable, and they can offer the support system to ensure every elder leads with strength. And while the elder is taking time to get their life on track, the church can move forward under the sound leadership of the remaining elders.

Keeping in mind this outline for elder selection, we will look next at the topic of authority and how it must be used by each elder.

6

Stewards of Authority

The Cult of "Power-Leadership"

IF YOU ARE READING this book, chances are you have been taken advantage of by a leader who abused their authority. The abuse may have been inside or outside the church, but you are not alone. I once had a boss who used his position to make all kinds of promises—promises he never intended to keep. He dangled the fictional carrot of "career advancement" to manipulate his employees and, in the process, he hurt both his reputation and the reputation of the company. Sadly, the church has too many leaders who model this same abuse of power . . . I have experienced it firsthand.

Roy Goble, at Red Letter Christian, summarizes well what may be considered the cult of leadership that has overtaken the church in the past thirty years. He writes,

> Sometimes it feels like a cult has formed around leadership. It's not just a church thing; it's prevalent in business, government, education, etc. You can see it everywhere. Authors try to come up with the next big leadership book. Speakers give us twelve steps to effective leadership. Seminars focus on the leader within us. Even "team" leadership becomes a buzzword.[1]

1. Goble, "Leadership as a Code Word."

Goble is right; leadership in much of the church has become simply a code word for power and that is not good. Even "team" has become a meaningless word in some circles. I am most grieved by one popular church-planting movement that claims to be built on a plurality of elders, yet through the use of terminology such as "executive elder" and "first among equals,"[2] they have turned the biblical concept of shared leadership into a system of one-man rule. The results, over time, have proven disastrous with some of the most prominent "firsts" abusing their power, seeking personal fame, and abusing the people. In one recent high-profile case, the list of charges against one "lead elder" by their "board of elders" included the following:[3]

- abandonment of genuine biblical community (Titus 1:8)
- refusal of personal accountability (failure to be a fellow elder according to 1 Pet 5:1)
- lack of self-control (1 Tim 3:2)

2. Black and McClung trace this terminology back to the second century and the birth of bishop rule. They write, "By the beginning of the second century, however, a new system gained acceptance on the ecclesiastical scene. In place of a pastoral board, a single overseer was set over his fellow elders as first-among-equals and was charged with oversight of the entire congregation. Properly concerned about the problems of heresy and disunity in the church—the same kind of problems Timothy faced in Ephesus—leaders like Ignatius of Antioch elevated the role of this single overseer to paramount importance. On his way to martyrdom in Rome in a.d. 107, Ignatius wrote seven letters to sister congregations, offering a simple but potentially far-reaching prescription for the ills of the church: obey the (one) bishop." Black and McClung, *1 & 2 Timothy*, 70. This moniker, "first among equals," eventually became synonymous with Roman popes (Galli and Olsen, introduction to *131 Christians Everyone Should Know*, 316), and emperors: "The first German emperor was Wilhelm I, king of Prussia. He served as primus inter pares (first among equals) with the heads of the other twenty-four states" (Metaxas, *Bonhoeffer*).

3. I am reticent to include the names of the fallen leaders as this tends to derail the conversation. Those with a morbid curiosity can search the internet for the bullet items listed, but I chose not to include the source to keep the argument from becoming an ad hominem. The failure is not alone with the man who succumbed to sin, it is the system the church has created that allows pastors to function as popes.

- manipulation and lying (Titus 1:8)
- domineering over those in his charge (1 Pet 5:3)
- misuse of power/authority (1 Pet 5:3)
- a history of building his identity through ministry and media platforms (necessity to be "sober-minded" in 1 Tim 3:2 and avoid selfish gain in 1 Pet 5:2).

These cases show that regardless of the titles we chose, the structure of the church's leaders matters. As Meisinger observes, "when one man arrogates to himself sole final authority in a church, he creates a dependent congregation, looking to him for all guidance and wisdom. He in practice may become an autocrat, a replicate pope."[4]

The problem is that in response to unhealthy leadership (leadership = power), we have turned to more unhealthy leadership models (no leaders = shared power). But in both cases, leadership is still being defined by its use, or non-use, of "power." The result of this emphasis on leadership is we often neglect other valuable metrics like wisdom, love, and joy.

Responding to the Abuse of Power

In reaction against this kind of abuse, some Christians have rejected both leadership and authority in the church. They claim, "only Jesus leads," and no man or woman should have any office or any authority over any other person. Wade Burleson, a pastor and president of Istoria Ministries, shares this view,

> There is no emphasis in the New Testament on authority that is derived from any "office" or position. Let me repeat that again: Nowhere in the New Testament does it say that a Christian, because of title or position, has moral authority over another Christian. The idea of an "office" of authority in the church, like that of the office of "President of the United States," simply does not exist.

4. Meisinger, "Elders: How Many?," 24.

> Christ alone has the position of authority in the church
> and He has no vicar on earth but His Spirit, who resides
> in the life of every believer.[5]

There are two distinct claims in this short passage that Burleson conflates that we must untangle. The first claim rejects all leadership and authority in the church, and is rather easy to dismiss. In addition to what has been previously written about elders in this book, the author of Hebrews tells us directly to honor leaders and respect their authority:

> Obey your leaders and submit to them, for they are
> keeping watch over your souls, as those who will have
> to give an account. Let them do this with joy and not
> with groaning, for that would be of no advantage to you.
> (Heb 13:17 ESV)

So if you come to the Scripture with an open mind and not ruled by the pain of the past, it is clear that God wants leaders to lead and he wants the church to respect their authority.

The second aspect of Burleson's statement is really the subject of this chapter; the abusive leadership system rooted in the Western business culture. Carl F. H. Henry has observed the pervasive and destructive tendencies of modern leadership:

> The problem of authority is one of the most deeply dis-
> tressing concerns of contemporary civilization. Anyone
> who thinks that this problem specially or exclusively em-
> barrasses Bible believers has not listened to the wild winds
> of defiance now sweeping over much of modern life.
> Respect for authority is being challenged on almost every
> front and in almost every form. . . . How to justify any
> human authority becomes an increasingly acute problem.
> Not only religious authority, but political, parental, and
> academic authority as well come under debate.[6]

The culture has rightly rejected abuse, but in so doing it has also tended to reject authority. The church must not fall into this

---

5. Burleson, "Our Problem Is Authoritarianism."
6. Henry, *God, Revelation, and Authority*, 4:7.

trap. The problem is not that we have leaders; the problem is we have corrupt leaders. The problem of authority is not that it exists; the problem is that authority is abused in defiance of what the Scripture teaches.

Jesus gives us one example of the call to lead and it is recorded for us in the book of Mark. In accord with both synagogue & Greco-Roman custom, Jesus' disciples began to jockey for status and power.[7] In response, Jesus calls his disciples to gather and he says to them,

> And Jesus called them to him and said to them, "You know that those who are considered rulers of the Gentiles lord it over them, and their great ones exercise authority over them. But it shall not be so among you. But whoever would be great among you must be your servant, and whoever would be first among you must be slave of all. For even the Son of Man came not to be served but to serve, and to give his life as a ransom for many." (Mark 10:42–45 ESV)

It is important to note that in this exchange with his disciples, Jesus was not critical of leadership nor did he condemn the use of authority. Jesus sought only to correct the disciples' perception of leadership and authority which was wrongly founded in the culture. A leader is a servant. A leader is humble. A leader in the kingdom of God models the sacrifice of Jesus.

Paul, like Jesus, had a vision for relational servant-leadership that challenged the status-quo of his day.[8] Dr. Joseph Hellerman in his book *Embracing Shared Ministry* makes this very point.

> Paul's goal was to create a very different kind of community among the followers of Jesus in first-century Philippi. The Philippian church was to be a community that discouraged competition for status and privilege, a place where the honor game was off-limits, in summary, a community in which persons with power and authority used their social capital not to further their own personal

7. Hellerman, *Embracing Shared Ministry*, 42.
8. Ibid., 118.

or familial agendas but, rather, to serve their brothers and sisters in Christ.[9]

In the letter to the church, Paul recognizes there are selfish leaders and generous leaders and regardless of their motive, he is thankful that the gospel is advancing (Phil 1:15–18). Yet, his hope was that both the elders and the people of the church would proclaim the gospel with a right motive. Paul hoped they would emulate his sacrifice and serve one another with humility.

> So if there is any encouragement in Christ, any comfort from love, any participation in the Spirit, any affection and sympathy, complete my joy by being of the same mind, having the same love, being in full accord and of one mind. Do nothing from selfish ambition or conceit, but in humility count others more significant than yourselves. Let each of you look not only to his own interests, but also to the interests of others. Have this mind among yourselves, which is yours in Christ Jesus, who, though he was in the form of God, did not count equality with God a thing to be grasped, but emptied himself, by taking the form of a servant, being born in the likeness of men. And being found in human form, he humbled himself by becoming obedient to the point of death, even death on a cross. (Phil 2:1–8 ESV, emphasis added)

The elder must be willing to lead the church by modeling the life of Jesus Christ. The elder must be willing to sacrifice his whole life, so that all God's people will grow mature in faith. This theme of loving-sacrifice pervades the writings of Paul. As Ben Witherington observes,

> No one who has read Galatians or 2 Corinthians carefully will doubt that Paul had a very high view of the authority and revelation granted to an apostle. He is not strictly egalitarian in his view of church leadership if by that one means non-hierarchical. He is quite clearly over many

9. Ibid., 119.

Gentiles, but he prefers to set an example, to lead by love and persuasion rather than by demand and command.[10]

The church needs leaders. The church needs leaders who rightly wield the authority of God. The church does not need any more leaders who model the abusive, power-hungry, and self-aggrandizing behaviors of the world.

Every Follower a Leader[11]

Several years ago I saw a funny little cartoon depicting an Egyptian master sitting atop a massive stone. He was whipping the slaves as they labored to pull this block to build a pyramid. The caption below the cartoon assured the slaves, "Believe me, fellows, everyone from the Pharaoh on down is an equally valued member of team."

We can all see how funny, and ridiculous, it is to suggest that these slaves were in any way equal to the Egyptian Pharaoh. Similarly, my suggestion that "every follower is a leader" in the church may seem just as silly, but I think it is biblical. To explain why this is a valid assertion, let's start with this functional definition of leadership.

> In the church family, every follower of Jesus is a member, every member is a minister and every minister is a leader.

First let me make a few observations about the term leadership.

- Leadership is not a job description, it is a character trait.

- Leadership is a demonstration of mature discipleship.

- Leadership is not synonymous with a church office (elder/deacon) or gifting from the Holy Spirit (pastor/teacher).

Years ago when I shared these thoughts to my congregation, my friend Marion asked a very insightful question:

---

10. Witherington, *Letters*, 265–66.

11. Adapted from my original article "Every Follower a Leader."

> So if I'm reading this correctly, Joe, everyone in the church family is a leader—or could be one, anyway. The reason why I say "could" is because not everyone "will" ... as a matter of fact I would say most do not see themselves as leaders in the traditional sense and are happy not to take on any leadership because with it comes increased responsibility, commitment and accountability within the church body.

Marion was totally right. It is tragic that not everyone will choose to become a leader, but still God's design for church is that every follower find a way to lead. And the job of an elder is to ensure everyone is recognized for their gifting in a way that will build up the family under the authority of Jesus Christ. Marion is a great example of how this works out.

As a young believer in our church, she experienced tremendous growth in her faith and it showed in her leadership. Marion was a mother and a great spiritual leader for her kids. Marion was a leader in our MOPS group and modeled what it meant to be a follower of Jesus to many of the younger moms. Marion worked with our kids on Sunday. Some of these kids do not have a stable home environment and Marion was able to lead these kids into a relationship with Jesus. Marion always took the initiative;

When there was a need . . . she stepped forward.

When the Holy Spirit moved . . . Marion listened, took action and modeled obedience to Christ.

That, to me, is the maturity of faith that defines leadership in the body of Christ. But with all this going for her, Marion still had trouble seeing herself as a leader. She once wrote to me,

> I don't think of myself as someone leading the church. In doing the things you've mentioned I live my life putting Christ front and center allowing the Holy Spirit to be in the "driver's seat" to ultimately bring Glory to God through His Grace. My goal every day is to live a surrendered life in the Spirit and therefore I don't lead, instead I'm being led.
>
> And only when I can let go of my selfish desire to be in control all the time (and boy what hard work that is) I

can touch the life of others in a way that God's Grace can shine through me.

I cannot take credit for something God has done, so I'd rather just look on with my brothers and sisters.

Wow! That is shared leadership and the heart of what makes a leader thrive. Marion's actions demonstrated to everyone that she was a leader and her attitude demonstrates why Marion was, and is, a great one!

But striving to let everyone lead, does not mean the church can function outside of divine authority. Shared leadership does not mean a rejection of elders. Early in the nineteenth century, many Southern Baptists pastors dealt with this same issue. Walter B. Shurden in his well-titled article "The Priesthood of All Believers and Pastoral Authority in Baptist Thought" makes the following observation:

> With Dagg and W. B. Johnson before him, Dargan emphasized that a plurality of elders existed in most New Testament congregations. These elders, Dargan believed, were accorded "a certain amount of authority," but it was "moral and executive rather than governmental or judicial." Relating pastoral authority to congregational authority in the Baptist churches of his days, Dargan observed, "the churches recognize these officers as executive only. The seat of authority is in the church, and to the church all its officers are directly responsible."[12]

Each congregation may draw the lines differently, but what is clear from both Scripture and tradition is that a plurality of elders leading the church is necessary, but in no way violates the priesthood of all believers who share in the leadership responsibilities. Shared leadership means that we put a greater value on every believer and not just a few of them.

---

12. Shurden, "Priesthood of All Believers," 35.

Five Keys to Practicing Divine Authority

Bad leadership is not the "other guy's" problem. Elders who abuse authority diminish the ability of everyone else to succeed as leaders. Men who embrace a true plurality tend to reject titles that set them above others, like "senior elder," "senior pastor," or "executive elder." Effective leaders, on the other hand, know how to succeed while using their authority to inspire others—not keep them down. So how can you become an elder who rightly handles authority? Paul continues to be a rich example.

Two thousand years ago, the Apostle Paul was a leader in the early Christian church and he was also in a battle for the hearts and minds of the Corinthian saints. Although you and I lead a different kind of church in a different cultural context, we can empathize with some of Paul's leadership troubles. The people were being misled and deceived by "strong" leaders who were eloquent speakers but abusive in practice.

Leaders who were zealous for power, saw Paul as a threat. To gain power, they painted Paul as an inferior apostle; in part because he was not a great speaker who chose a bi-vocational lifestyle, and also because he did not have a strong charismatic presence. Paul was criticized as a physically ill-person who could not heal himself, and consequently his credentials as a true apostle of Jesus were questioned. Paul spoke strong words in his letters, but in person, they charged, he lacked that same boldness. Paul's detractors spun the facts to diminish Paul as a respected leader.

In his response to these corrupt leaders, Paul attempted to refine the Corinthian's thinking so they could discern divine authority from abusive authority; good leaders from bad leaders. In reading chapter 10 of Paul's second letter to the Corinthian church, I see five keys to help elders properly practice authority.

1. Divine Authority Is Not Exclusive

> Look at what is before your eyes. If anyone is confident that he is Christ's, let him remind himself that just as he

> is Christ's, so also are we. For even if I boast a little too
> much of our authority, which the Lord gave for building
> you up and not for destroying you, I will not be ashamed.
> (2 Cor 10:7–8 ESV)

Abusive leaders are always looking to create a "second-in-command" who will make them look better and do their bidding. In stark contrast, good leaders recognize authority is God's and they share it with other God-ordained leaders. In Paul's context, he never claimed to be "the" only apostle of Jesus. Notice in the passage above he speaks of "our" authority and how it was demonstrated in humility. And even if he had come across a little prideful, it was always for the benefit of the church.

2. Divine Authority Builds Up

> I do not want to appear to be frightening you with my
> letters. For they say, "His letters are weighty and strong,
> but his bodily presence is weak, and his speech of no ac-
> count." Let such a person understand that what we say
> by letter when absent, we do when present. Not that
> we dare to classify or compare ourselves with some of
> those who are commending themselves. But when they
> measure themselves by one another and compare them-
> selves with one another, they are without understanding.
> (2 Cor 10:9–12 ESV)

Corrupt leaders use their authority to elevate themselves in the eyes of others. They use their power to build their image and show their superiority over anyone else who dares to challenge their authority. In contrast, Paul says the right use of authority builds up others and is not used to tear them down. Leaders—confident in their authority—do not fear "competition." They encourage respect for the authority of others and teach people how to become strong leaders.

3. Divine Authority Is Built on "People" Accomplishment

> Not that we dare to classify or compare ourselves with some of those who are commending themselves. But when they measure themselves by one another and compare themselves with one another, they are without understanding. But we will not boast beyond limits, but will boast only with regard to the area of influence God assigned to us, to reach even to you. For we are not overextending ourselves, as though we did not reach you. For we were the first to come all the way to you with the gospel of Christ. (2 Cor 10:12–14 ESV)

Abusive leaders are always giving you their resume because they fear you won't otherwise obey their authority. They feel the need to diminish the accomplishments of others so their successes look bigger. Bad leadership is built on a resume of "personal" accomplishments. These leaders seek out followers who are humble and giving so they can take more. The leader who boasts in their own successes as a reason to trust their authority will usually end up abusing it. In contrast, the biblical leader builds on "people" accomplishment. That is, his success is measured in the lives of others and their faithfulness to Jesus Christ.

4. Divine Authority Rejoices in the Success of Others

> We do not boast beyond limit in the labors of others. But our hope is that as your faith increases, our area of influence among you may be greatly enlarged. (2 Cor 10:15 ESV)

A bad leader will point to how big their church is, how much money they made, how many academic degrees they have earned, or how many books they have published as their source of authority. In stark contrast, a good leader points to the lives of people they have encouraged, strengthened, and propelled to success as the demonstration of their right use of authority.

5. Divine Authority Comes from God

> We do not boast beyond limit in the labors of others. But our hope is that as your faith increases, our area of influence among you may be greatly enlarged, so that we may preach the gospel in lands beyond you, without boasting of work already done in another's area of influence. "Let the one who boasts, boast in the Lord." For it is not the one who commends himself who is approved, but the one whom the Lord commends. (2 Cor 10:15–18 ESV)

Finally, a good leader does not abuse their authority by taking the credit for the work others have done. A good leader celebrates every individual for their accomplishment and builds strong teams that can do great things. Why? Because they know that their authority comes from God and they do not fear the success of others. As Benjamin Merkle observes,

> The authority of the eldership comes from God and not the congregation. Although the congregation affirms the elders' calling and authority, theirs is an authority with a divine origin. Paul tells the Ephesian elders that the Holy Spirit made them overseers (Acts 20:28). They were called and given authority by God and not by man.[13]

A leader confident in their God-given authority is not afraid that others may gain from their good work. On the contrary, he or she shares the credit so that others can succeed. Ultimately, a good leader knows that the only commendation they need comes from God himself; the God who is the source of all authority in the church.

As William Secker sadly observed, "great men's vices are more imitated than poor men's graces." This is the way of the world, but should not be the way of the church. Let us as elders, seek to emulate the right leaders who demonstrate divine authority so that we too might receive the commendation of God.

---

13. Merkle, *Why Elders?*, Kindle loc. 314–16.

7

Financial Support

IN MY LIFETIME OF service to the church, I have played many parts and been blessed financially in different ways. I put aside a potentially profitable career in engineering and turned down an offer of a six-figure salary to honor God's call to a full-time ministry. Over the years I have been paid to work both full time, and part time, and as a church planter I work bi-vocationally. At times I have given of myself without any financial benefit and in some cases I have been blessed with a simple honorarium. The question becomes, "are any one of these actions more 'biblical' than the other?"

Based on my previous chapter on qualities of an elder, we know that an elder is a servant-leader who is not ruled by the love of money. At the same time, Paul makes clear that elders have the right to receive financial support from the church.

> Let the elders who rule well be considered worthy of double honor, especially those who labor in preaching and teaching. For the Scripture says, "You shall not muzzle an ox when it treads out the grain," and, "The laborer deserves his wages." (1 Tim 5:17–18 ESV)

William D. Mounce in his commentary on 1 Timothy explains how this passage fits into Paul's general rule of churches supporting elders who shared the teaching responsibilities.

Paul begins the first of his four statements about elders on the same note with which he began and ended the preceding discussion of widows—honor—and in both cases honor involves money. The elders who were following his instructions and doing a good job not only were worthy of the peoples' respect but should also be paid for their work ("double honor"). He will continue in v. 18 with his reason: workers should be paid. This was Paul's general rule (1 Cor 9:4–6; cf. Rom 13:7) although he himself often chose to earn his own living (cf. 1 Cor 4:12; 2 Cor 11:7–9; 1 Thess 2:9; cf. 2 Thess 3:7–9; Acts 18:3).[1]

So what we have so far is a clear biblical teaching connected with historical examples of men, ordained by the Spirit, receiving financial blessing for their ministry to the church. A deeper examination of the history through the eyes of New Testament scholar and historian Dr. Ben Witherington affirms this conclusion. Building upon the cultural expectation of hospitality that a workman is worth his hire, and Paul's unique application of it among the Corinthian Christians, Witherington makes clear that the elder/pastor found worthy has the right to receive support from his congregation.[2]

What we see then is a scriptural corroboration and a consistency of actions over time which support the concept of elders receiving money from the church. Keeping this in mind, there are a few important things to remember before we apply this to our churches today.

First, I have noticed a disturbing trend in the writings of some men and women on this subject. There is a tendency to emphasize Paul's example of tentmaking while ignoring the other periods of his ministry when he lived on the support of churches alone.[3]

Second, despite Paul's personal choice to serve bi-vocationally, Paul's teaching about elders, based on our previous guidelines, has a greater authority for the church. Paul was an apostle, not an

1. Mounce, *Pastoral Epistles*, 306.

2. Witherington, "Pagan Christianity." See also Matt 10:10; 1 Cor 9:14; 2 Cor 11:7ff.

3. Acts 18:1–5.

elder, and so his actions provide a model of sacrificial-service that should be respected by all Christians. However, the church must give priority to his direct teaching on how to financially support her teaching elders.

Third, everything examined so far demonstrates that elders in the early church did receive financial support from the local church and this support was in alignment with God's design for the New Testament church. But, how does this translate into the modern church paying a salary to an elder?

In point of fact, there is no direct "apples to apples" correlation between the early church's application of the cultural expectation of hospitality and the modern church's cultural expectation of a salary. Alan Knox, at the end of a long series on this topic, concludes,

> The difficulty is that there is no specific passage in Scripture that either commands or forbids salaries for elders/ pastors. There is no "smoking gun," if you will. . . . Thus, any position that someone might hold on this topic would be derived from many different passages. And, that's why it is important to study all of the evidence.[4]

Mounce elaborates on this point in his commentary on the Pastoral Epistles:

> While itinerant missionaries (such as the apostles) did receive payment, elders working in their local churches received not a salary but an honorarium "on a person-to-person and day-to-day basis, according to the circumstances, . . . [and] above all it is a free-will offering, the very antithesis to a regular paid salary." . . .
>
> (1) It is unlikely that the early church would have had sufficient funds to pay a regular salary; (2) 1 Tim 3:7 suggests that elders retained their jobs in the secular world; (3) τιμή means "honorarium" and never "regular salary"; and (4) "it does not seem likely that Paul would make a regular salary dependent on some sort of efficiency test . . . because of the sure threat of division it would bring."[5]

---

4. Knox, "Vocational Pastor."

5. Mounce, *Pastoral Epistles*, 309.

These are good arguments, with some historical assumptions, and a fair summary of the issue. However, just because these two practices, the NT honorarium vs. modern salary, are unique in form, does not mean the modern salary is unbiblical or pagan.

For example, the New Testament period knew nothing of our modern healthcare system, so the form in which the church might choose to care for the physical needs of her elders, or of any member of the church for that matter, can be very different than in the first-century church or churches around the globe. There is no early church record of a church providing a parsonage, yet in many groups this is an acceptable way to care for their pastors.

Let me offer one last passage that has bearing on this discussion and then I will offer a summary. We can learn an important lesson from Paul's teaching to the church at Rome on making false judgements about what practices have no place in the church.

> Therefore let us not pass judgment on one another any longer, but rather decide never to put a stumbling block or hindrance in the way of a brother. I know and am persuaded in the Lord Jesus that nothing is unclean in itself, but it is unclean for anyone who thinks it unclean. For if your brother is grieved by what you eat, you are no longer walking in love. By what you eat, do not destroy the one for whom Christ died. So do not let what you regard as good be spoken of as evil. For the kingdom of God is not a matter of eating and drinking but of righteousness and peace and joy in the Holy Spirit. Whoever thus serves Christ is acceptable to God and approved by men. So then let us pursue what makes for peace and for mutual upbuilding. Do not, for the sake of food, destroy the work of God. Everything is indeed clean, but it is wrong for anyone to make another stumble by what he eats. It is good not to eat meat or drink wine or do anything that causes your brother to stumble. The faith that you have, keep between yourself and God. Blessed is the one who has no reason to pass judgment on himself for what he approves. But whoever has doubts is condemned if he eats, because the eating is not from faith. For whatever does not proceed from faith is sin. (Rom 14:13–23 ESV, emphasis added)

Taking into account the Scriptures, important cultural concerns, and applying the guidelines outlined in the last chapter, we can make a proper application of the apostolic teaching to our modern context without doing violence to the church or Scripture.

Instructions to the Churches

Salaries Are Not Un-biblical

Although elders in the early church did not receive a salary as we know it today, there is no biblical prohibition against it. At the same time, there is no biblical foundation for thinking only a full-time paid elder can lead the church. Regardless of pay, there is no such thing as lay or clergy. All elders are equal in their authority, and ministry.

The Church Is Free to Decide

Elders who receive a full-time salary are in line with Scripture; but, so too are elders who receive a part-time salary, no salary, a parsonage, healthcare, or only the occasional honorarium. It is at the discretion of each church to decide on how to honor their elders. At the same time, it is wrong for others to despise the liberty of the church. The condemnation from Pharisaical-outsiders who pretend to have authority not given by YHWH should find no place among God's people.

There Are No Limits on Generosity

A church that withholds all forms of financial support from her elders is in violation of the biblical norm and apostolic expectation.[6] As a matter of fact, there is no moral or biblical limitation on the generosity of a church toward her elders, and therefore

---

6. See 1 Tim 5:17–18.

anyone from the outside who tries to limit the generosity of the local church is acting against the Scripture.

So what is the "proper" and "biblical" way to financially compensate an elder in the church? There is none! A church in China is not the same as a church in California. A church in West Virginia is not the same as a church in Mexico. God has given both discretion and freedom to the church and the Holy Spirit must lead each family to decide how to properly honor their elders.

Instructions to the Elders

Elders Must Be Generous

Circumstances within the church change; and there are times when an elder must lay aside his right to compensation so that he can better serve the family. Elders should not let tradition determine how much they accept, but they must do what is right for the church above their own need.

Eldest Must Serve the Gospel above Money

Within certain communities and cultures, even in the West, taking a salary could hinder the proclamation of the gospel, and each elder must make a decision to accept or reject a church's honorarium based on what is best for the kingdom.

Elders Should Not Be for Hire

The church's ability to pay a salary should not determine the calling of an elder. Elders should not seek to serve the highest bidder or treat the calling of elder as a job where one works their way up the ladder of corporate success.

Let's sum up each of these points by looking at the example of Paul. Although not an elder, Paul provides an example of how times and circumstances can change the elder's approach to money.

> After this Paul left Athens and went to Corinth. And he found a Jew named Aquila, a native of Pontus, recently come from Italy with his wife Priscilla, because Claudius had commanded all the Jews to leave Rome. And he went to see them, and because he was of the same trade he stayed with them and worked, for they were tentmakers by trade. And he reasoned in the synagogue every Sabbath, and tried to persuade Jews and Greeks. When Silas and Timothy arrived from Macedonia, Paul was occupied with the word, testifying to the Jews that the Christ was Jesus. (Acts 18:1–5 ESV)

At times, Paul supported himself as a tent-maker and at other times he relied solely on the financial support of the church. Sometimes Paul struggled and other times he had more than enough (Phil 4:12–13). Paul's course was never determined by his need, but by his mission to serve the gospel and so it should be with our elders.

With the issue of pastoral salaries behind us, let's move on to apply the previous guidelines to the issue of leadership structures for the church.

8

Abandon the CEO Structure

WITHOUT QUESTION, THE ROLE, and expectation, of being a pastor in America has changed in the past hundred years. Read along as Gordon MacDonald recalls this conversation with his father.

> My father had been a successful pastor in his younger years, a hero to more than a few in his time. So in the first years of my pastoral life, I measured myself against him. I'd think, when my father was my age, he was preaching to seven hundred people. I'm preaching to only one hundred. What's wrong with me?
>
> Later on, I found myself in a congregation several times the size of his largest, and I remember having an empty feeling. I'd exceeded his numbers. Why didn't I feel better about it? And why was I now measuring myself against someone else (always with bigger numbers)?
>
> One day my dad and I were comparing notes about the contrasts between his ministry and mine.
>
> "You guys have to worry about so many programs today," he said. "You are all glorified CEOs. There's not a one of you in these large churches who can honestly call himself a pastor. Pastors care for people; you run programs and build institutions."
>
> "You didn't worry about programs?" I asked.
>
> "Oh, there were a few," he said.
>
> "How many?"
>
> "Basically three," he answered.

"Three?" I was leading a church that had 137 programs (we counted them one time), and he had only three?

"Yeah, three," he said. "I was responsible for Sunday services, calling on people during the week, and leading the prayer service on Wednesday night. I spent my time with the sick, the unsaved, and the men who were trying to build strong families."

"What about Christian education?" I wondered.

"Some of the women took care of that."

"Didn't they bring you their recruitment problems, their circular debates, all their—"

"No, none of that was considered a pastor's responsibility. I told you; I led people to Christ, called on the sick, and every once in a while, had to go out to the local bar and bring a drunk home to his wife and help him sober up."

Maybe my dad was right. The new CEO pastor is a marketer, a manager, a publicist, a systems analyzer, a small-groups mobilizer.

Then again, the pastor is expected to communicate like Campolo, lead like Criswell, think like Packer, and theologize like Stott, be prophetic like Colson, and evangelize like Graham.

Perhaps we've made a dangerous move by sizing up ourselves on the basis of our ability to grow large, impressive organizations. We hear less and less about the quality of a leader's spirit. The conferences—for the most part—are all about the "market," the institution, the program.

Perhaps this is not all bad, except when it is compared with the amount of time on the subject of soul and its capacity to be prophetic, perceptive, and powerful.[1]

These same themes are picked up by many contemporary observers of the church. Compare what you read about elders earlier in this book with this observation of the CEO-pastor from Os Guinness.

---

1. Dunnam et al., *Mastering Personal Growth*, 174.

Look at church-growth literature and check for such chapters as "Portrait of the Effective Pastor." In one such best-seller, theology and theological references are kept to a minimum—little more than a cursory reference to the pastor's "personal calling" and to "God's vision for the church." The bulk of the chapter is taken up with such themes as delegating, confidence, interaction, decision making, visibility, practicality, accountability, and discernment—the profile of the thoroughly modern pastor as CEO.[2]

Now before we react against this observation and think the problem is one of size, we must think again. Large or small, mega or mini; the unhealthy demands placed on today's pastor come in all shapes and sizes. The pressures placed on elders have grown, in part, because churches of every size have adopted structures that resemble the modern American corporation where the pastor presides as the CEO. There are two unique models that really fall under this rubric of "CEO structure." The first model has the pastor sitting alone at the top of the hierarchy of leadership.

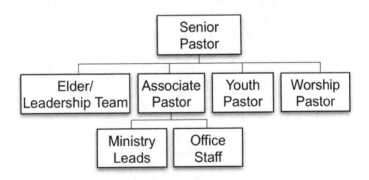

The chart above reflects the typical leadership structure in most Evangelical churches in the United States. This model certainly finds its roots in the modern corporate business structure, but may even go back further to the second century. Benjamin

2. Guinness, *Dining with the Devil*, 52–53.

Merkle writes how this special class of CEO pastor is so destructive to the life of the church.

> By creating a "professional" class of elders (i.e., pastors or senior pastors), we create an unhealthy and unbiblical distinction. Nowhere in the Bible are elders who work "full time" for the church given a different title than those elders who also hold a "secular" job. Such a distinction creates an unhealthy dichotomy between the full-time and part-time elders, as well as between the clergy and laity. By speaking of a "senior pastor," in essence, we have created a third office, similar to what took place in the second century with the development of the monarchical bishop.[3]

Another form of this CEO structure is found among congregational churches and is defined by Wayne Grudem.

> [Some congregational models are] patterned after the example of a modern corporation, where the board of directors hires an executive officer who then has authority to run the business as he sees fit. This form of government could also be called the "you-work-for-us" structure. In favor of this structure it might be argued that this system in fact works well in contemporary businesses. However, there is no New Testament precedent or support for such a form of church government. It is simply the result of trying to run the church like a modern business, and it sees the pastor not as a spiritual leader, but merely as a paid employee.[4]

The above description of the corporate board model may be illustrated as follows:

---

3. Merkle, *40 Questions*, Kindle loc. 528–31.
4. Grudem, *Systematic Theology*, 935.

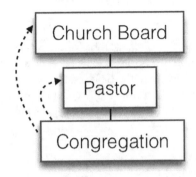

There are many viable environments, different culturally conditioned methods, and a variety of structures through which biblical elders can lead a church. However, this does not mean all structures are equally beneficial in growing a strong family. So before I offer my critique, let me be clear where I part company with some contemporary Christian writers.

- Churches who use these CEO models are not evil.

- Pastors who minister within this model are not the enemy of the church.

- We should not vilify any pastor who does church with this model nor should we blame them for all the shortcomings of the American church.

- One's singular dislike of this model is not a compelling reason to leave a church or reject fellowship with people who worship Jesus in these churches.

- The gospel can, and is, preached without compromise in churches that exist using this structure of ministry.

That being said, I do think that the "pastor as CEO" model is a cultural adaptation that has, over time, demonstrated some grave weaknesses that we, the church, must take seriously and that we must work together to correct. The pastor as CEO model is not one that is found in the New Testament church. As Stott observes,

> There is no biblical warrant either for the one-man band
> (a single pastor playing all the instruments of the orches-
> tra himself) or for a hierarchical or pyramidal structure
> in the local church (a single pastor perched at the apex
> of the pyramid). On the contrary, the church had a plural
> oversight from the beginning.[5]

Based on my personal experience, here are a few of the draw-backs I have observed in churches that use this structure of church leadership.

- The structure looks less like a family and more like a company and therefore tends to put the interests of the institution above the interests of the individual.

- The pastor as CEO model tends to focus on the man at the top instead of the mission for the people.

- This model puts enormous responsibility on one man (typically called the senior pastor but the title is of secondary importance) who more often than not gets burned out or burned over.

- This model can isolate and hurt the senior pastor who does not have the proper support or accountability from his peers (i.e., brothers in Christ).

My concern is not just for the churches, but also for the men who serve as elders in a system that can harm their own spiritual maturity. For now, I will move forward and focus on some different approaches to church leadership that both value elders as spiritual big brothers and the church as a family.[6]

---

5. Stott, "Ideals of Pastoral Ministry," 68. Adapted from Stott, "Christian Ministry in the 21st Century Part 4," 4.

6. For further reading, see Wagner, *Escape from Church, Inc.*, 256.

9

Embrace the Missional Structure

The Synagogue vs. the Church

THE SERVICE OF THE Christian elder has roots in our Jewish heritage, but it also has characteristics unique to the New Covenant. A quick study of just one of these differences between Old and New tells a lot about God's missional design for the New Covenant church.

The synagogue structure, which was headed by a president who ruled over the elders, chancellor and the alms givers, strongly resembles the pastor-CEO structure we examined in the previous chapter. David Miller's description can be illustrated as follows:[1]

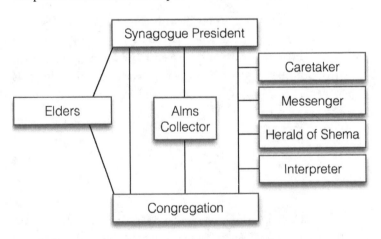

1. Miller, "Uniqueness of the New Testament Church Eldership," 323.

In contrast to the synagogue ruled by a monarchial president, "[the New Testament] local church has a simple two-level organizational structure of a plurality of elders and a plurality of deacons (Phil 1:1)."[2]

So why then did the apostles embrace some synagogue traditions (such as elders) and, in the case of overall structure and ritualistic observances, make such a radical departure from their Jewish brethren?[3] Because they recognized, through divine revelation, that the old Jewish form of presidential leadership would restrict the spread of the gospel in several ways.

1. The synagogue model relied on the civil and political power of the president, and was therefore less adaptable to diverse and changing cultures.[4]

2. The synagogue model hinders rapid growth and expansion because there are fewer leaders modeling and equipping the younger in faith.

3. The synagogue model has a limited attraction because it only draws in people who connect with the president.

Therefore, the apostles established the church using a missional structure, which included elders, that could change, grow, morph and adapt to the needs of each culture.[5]

2. Ibid., 324.

3. Mappes writes, "While most scholars agree that the church borrowed the concept of πρεσβύτερος from the Jewish synagogue, they disagree on the similarities between the Jewish synagogal eldership and church eldership. Some scholars, such as Rayburn, argue for a complete analogous relationship between the church and the synagogue, while others argue for a relationship in name only. The present writer concludes that while the church is distinct from the synagogue, there are enough similarities between them to substantiate the synagogal influence on the early church." See Mappes, "'Elder' in the Old and New Testaments," 80. Adapted from Mappes, "'Elder' in the Old and New Testaments," 89.

4. Ibid., 81.

5. Morey has an insightful chapter that also includes a long discussion of the role of women in church leadership through the first few centuries of the church. He writes, "The Church's dynamic approach to positions of honor and ministry enabled it to transcend all cultural boundaries. While being careful

Andrew Kirk, as quoted by Vencer in his article "The Ministry of Management for Christian Workers," gives six principles of Christian ministry.[6]

1. No distinction either in form, language or theory between clergy and laity was ever accepted by the New Testament church.

2. The ministry is coextensive with the entire church (1 Cor 12:7).

3. The local church in the apostolic age always functioned under a plurality of leadership.

4. There are no uniform models for ministry in the New Testament; the patterns are flexible and versatile.

5. In the New Testament church can be found both leadership and authority, but no kind of hierarchical structure.

6. There is one, and only one, valid distinction which the New Testament appears to recognize within the ministry, apart from the different functions to which we have been alluding: the distinction between local and itinerant ministries.

Vencer goes on to conclude that although the church eventually moved away from this early practice, their early leadership structure was clearly in favor of shared leadership.

> The norm of church rule was plurality and shared leadership. This may understandably have been so because the church was a "new creation" and the apostles had no existing pattern of leadership to follow. While the fact of government in church was evident, still no biblical form was described. The church had the freedom to evolve within the general framework of church polity.[7]

---

to maintain such supra-cultural permanent offices as elder and deacon, the Church can set up culturally conditioned positions as a valid way to relate to every culture and civilization." See Morey, *Encyclopedia of Practical Christianity*, 424.

6. Vencer, "Ministry of Management," 292–93.

7. Ibid.

It should be noted that while the apostles eschewed the tradition of the synagogue president, the establishment of a missional structure using a plurality of elders was not a rejection of all authority or leadership in the church.

> That the church is to have leadership is a Divine requirement (Heb. 13:7, 17). Organization is not wrong or carnal. People go to extremes on this matter. Some feel that the less organization the better, though in practice the work is hindered by not having sufficient organization. Others go to the other extreme and are so highly organized that it is difficult, if not impossible, for the Head of the church to be heard.[8]

Missional Is Not a Rejection of Structure

Nelson Searcy was in the Portland area a few years back for a seminar on evangelism and church growth. If you are not familiar with Nelson, he is the lead pastor for the Journey Church in New York City and runs several networks to train pastors through his Church Leader Insights. As part of the seminar, a bunch of us sat down for a round-table discussion and began a conversation about systems in the church.

To those of us who are intrigued by "organic" church growth, the idea of systems can leave us cold. Yet, as the conversation progressed, Nelson used a wonderful analogy that helped me reconcile my own internal conflict between the world of "organic" with the world of "structure." Expanding on Nelson's analogy, I put together some thoughts on how systems work within the church organism.

The human body is an organism made up of many different parts; hands, feet, head, heart, appendix, etc. None of these parts can function well unless they are connected together with healthy systems. What are some of the systems that keep the individual parts of our bodies healthy? With the help of *Wikipedia*, I offer these simple definitions.

---

8. Ryrie, *Survey of Bible Doctrine*, electronic ed.

- The Skeletal System: Determines the shape of the body and protects the organs.

- The Circulatory System: A collection of organs that moves nutrients, gases, and wastes, helps fight disease, and stabilizes both temperature and pH to keep the body stable.

- The Digestive System: An arrangement of organs that takes in food, digests it to extract energy and nutrients, and expels the remaining waste.

- The Reproductive System: An arrangement of organs within the body that work together for the purpose of creating new human beings.

- The Endocrine System: An integrated system of small organs that involve the release of hormones. (Okay, this system reminds me of my old jr. high youth group—enough said.)

When these systems shut down, the human body begins to die. In the same way, the church is an organic entity that demands healthy systems to keep it from dying.

What are some of the systems that keep our local church bodies healthy?

The Organizational System: Every church, from house church to mega-church, has some kind of organizational structure. An organizational system is like the skeletal system. The pastors, elders, paid staff, deacons, apostles, overseers, etc.; all work to give the body shape and offer both spiritual and physical protection (Acts 6:1–7 is one good example).

The Leadership System: The leadership system determines how leaders connect with the rest of God's people. A leadership system is like the circulatory system. A healthy leadership system filters out the waste, responds to the heartbeat of YHWH, and enables the individual parts of the body to imbibe the life giving "nutrients" of Jesus Christ. And just like the veins in our human bodies, the more servant-leaders in a church, the healthier the body will be.

The Assimilation System: The sssimilation system moves people from outside the church into fully committed participants of the local church. A system for assimilation is like the digestive system. A healthy assimilation system ensures that every person involved in the church is using their Spirit-giftings, and talents, to nourish the body.

The Evangelism System: The evangelism system enables the body to fulfill the great calling of Christ to make disciples. A system for evangelism is like the human reproductive system. The evangelism system connects all the members of the body and uses their energy to create new life in Jesus Christ.

These are just four of the organic body systems that come to mind, but there are many more.

A clear understanding and healthy use of systems is biblical, and it enables the natural growth of the church. Anyone who is planting and/or leading a church without the necessary systems is not building a viable church.

So while systems and structures are necessary, we must keep in mind that the simple mission of the church is not something we fulfill through systems or programs. Allowing the elders, deacons, mature disciples, staff, etc. . . . to take the lead, model the incarnational-life of Christ, and equip every person to fulfill the simple mission of the church is the start of a healthy structure. Like a ripple in a pond, leadership must live the Spirit-filled life of Christ and inspires others to reveal, to love and to abide in the good news of Jesus Christ.

This missional structure is a positive reflection of the principles I have outlined throughout this book and the emphasis is on the following four elements.

1. The church is the divine family with one God and Father over all.

2. The family as a living group instead of a legal organization.

3. Eliminate structures that hinder mission; build structures that empower people.

4. Build a church driven by divine mission, not by organizational hierarchy, personalities, or personal agendas.

The marks of a healthy missional structure are demonstrated in how the church lives out the eight qualities below.[9]

1. Spirit-Gifted Service

2. Need-Oriented Evangelism

3. Empowering Leadership

4. Inspiring Worship

5. Relational Structures

6. Loving Relationships

7. Passionate Spirit-Life

8. Holistic Small Groups

Now that we can see the missional structure of an elder-led family, my next chapter will add one last component of structure that places relationship over institution.

9. For a further discussion of these eight qualities, see the research from Schwartz, Natural Church Development, 128.

10

Live the Relational Structure

As DISCUSSED EARLIER, THE pastor as CEO model of ministry has some drawbacks when it comes to developing healthy relationships. I appreciated this summary comment Brent made on Alan Knox's blog, *The Assembling of the Church.*

> In my experience the role of pastor in our culture follows one of three patterns found in the business world: pastor as an employee, pastor as a CEO, and pastor as a sole proprietor. If the pastor is your employee you can be friends with him, but ultimately you have to evaluate his performance and may have to fire him. The relationship is limited by the burden of that constraint. If the pastor is a CEO he has to balance the demands and desires from several competing departments and granting access to certain people over others has political dimensions and creates resentment in those who don't have access to the decision maker. If the pastor is a sole proprietor he owns the "church" and runs it as a lifestyle business. You can be friends with him, but you need to do the things he wants in order to get along or you will no longer have a place in his business.[1]

The solution is to make sure that when we structure our churches, we do so in a way that reflects our value for biblical relationship and respect for the priesthood of all believers.[2]

1. Quoted from comments section of article, Knox, "One of Us."
2. 1 Pet 2:5.

First and foremost, we begin with a recognition that relationship begins with Jesus who sits at the right hand of God as the shepherd of the church—the groom who awaits his perfect bride.

No man—no elder—can replace Jesus, so while we wait for Jesus to come and gather his church, the Holy Spirit lives among and within her. The Spirit gives giftings to the people so that the whole body may grow in unity. Elders are the under-shepherds, who must rule well and administer the church and protect the flock until the appointed day of the Lord. As mentioned earlier, a plurality of elders over the church is the ideal biblical directive and practice.

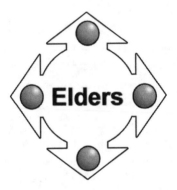

The diagram above is not concerned with the titles people choose to use, but the relationship shared by each elder represented by each of the dots. Every church and tradition will have a variety of names for different roles people play. The diversity of tradition is as great as the diversity of the body and no effort should be made to force everyone to follow one specific nomenclature.

The importance goes beyond titles and revolves around two things:

1. What does the elder do?

2. Who does he do it with?

The elders who rule well do not form a hierarchy of power, but they serve in relationship as a community within a community.

They serve as a model of what it means to be the hands and feet and voice of Jesus Christ. The four benefits of this approach are summarized well in this article by David J. MacLeod:

> First, it complements the church's nature as a family of brothers and sisters. A plural Eldership, unlike a formal clerical structure with its special titles, sacred clothes, chief seats, and lordly terminology, best expresses the church's character as a brotherhood.
>
> Second, it complements the church's nature as a non-clerical community. The New Testament knows nothing of a consecrated class of clerics who carry out the ministry for the laymen. Instead, every member of the church is a holy saint (1 Cor. 1:2), a royal priest (1 Pet. 2:5–10), and a Spirit-gifted member of the body of Christ (1 Cor. 12; Eph. 4:12).
>
> Third, the plural Eldership complements the church's nature as a humble-servant community. When it functions properly, shared leadership manifests mutual regard for one another, submission to one another, patience with one another, consideration of one another's interests, and deference to one another.
>
> Finally, plural Eldership complements the church's nature by guarding and promoting the preeminence and position of Christ over the local assembly. The apostles practiced a form of church government that reflected the distinctive, fundamental truth that Christ was the Ruler, Head, Lord, and Pastor of the church. "There is only one flock and one Pastor (John 10:16), one body and one Head (Col. 1:18), one holy priesthood and one great High Priest (Heb. 4:14–16), one brotherhood and one Older Brother (Rom. 8:29), one building and one Cornerstone (1 Pet. 2:5–8), one Mediator, one Lord. Jesus Christ is 'Senior Pastor,' and all others are His undershepherds (1 Pet. 5:4)."[3]

How then do we apply this relational structure to our modern churches of the West? The following diagram illustrates then how the leadership of the church no longer works from top-to-bottom

3. MacLeod, "Primacy of Scripture," 76–77.

but from inside-out. Each elder then becomes responsible for mentoring, guiding, and building the next generation of disciples through the use of deacons.

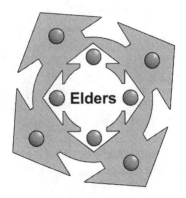

In some churches, they may find that one elder in particular is specially gifted to lead and organize the deacons. In another church, there may be several who share that specific role. The importance here is not in what titles we choose, but that we embrace the diversity of giftings among the elders and allow their diversity to make the church stronger. As we embrace God's design for a healthy family, there are a few points of application that I think important for the current debate about church.

1. Churches can meet in and own buildings; but they must not compromise their relational structure.

2. Churches can hire staff and use whatever titles they prefer; but they must not compromise their relational structure.

3. Churches can run programs and put on community events; but they must not compromise their relational structure.

With an understanding of both our missional and relational structures outlined in the previous chapters, the next chapter will explore elders as the catalyst for growing a strong community.

11

Become a Community Catalyst

EVER SINCE I WAS a teenager in ministry, I have believed that success is determined by how much I am not needed. I don't mean to suggest I have not struggled with other priorities, but as I look back on my life, this theme of growing strong replacements comes up again and again.

When I was doing initiative evangelism with Campus Crusade for Christ, I only felt totally successful when I taught someone else how to do what I was doing. When I was in youth ministry, I believed success would come only when I mentored someone to take my place and do what I was doing. When I teach a class or preach, I am always looking for that Spirit-gifted someone whom I can train for the future. In my church plants, I pray continually that God will bring men[1] who are called to plant so I can invest in them and send them out to plant more churches. When one role is filled by a gifted and equipped disciple, I move on to the next work and begin the process over again.

---

1. I only refer to men in this particular sentence because my emphasis here is on the people I personally disciple and mentor. As a man, I do not want to open myself to developing an improper relationship with a woman who is not my wife. So, out of respect for my wife and to protect my ministry, I will teach classes or do training in mixed gender groups, but always leave the discipleship of women to other strong women. Women are an important part of God's plan to plant churches and grow his church and I am thankful for the many amazing women in my life I can trust to build that next generation of female leaders.

The problem for many people I know in pastoral ministry is that their self-worth is attached to how much they are needed instead of how many people they have brought to maturity of faith. This unfortunate tendency fosters a system where one man sits at the top doing everything and is constantly needed by everyone. It leads to stress, isolation, and burnout. It leads to a church that cannot survive without the one man who leads. Eventually the pastor leaves, and the church is left to flounder. Yet even in these crippled congregations, there are people still gifted by the Spirit, but their muscles have atrophied for lack of use. So they sit, and wait, for someone else to get hired and take charge of the church and do the work of ministry. Robert Peterson expands on this theme as he expands on the lessons of history.

> One-man rule is very natural, for there are few natural leaders. The process is usually gradual, and this leader may not even consciously desire it. He takes charge because "no one else is doing the job." This type of rule can occur in spite of the fact that there is nominally an oversight or Eldership in the meeting. It sometimes happens when an eager person senses that the nominal leadership is doing little leading or shepherding. It can also happen with a person who feels a need to be in charge. One-man rule in an assembly is the result of a breakdown of leadership. But we should not be quick to blame that person alone. It is the rest of the Elders who have relinquished their responsibility by letting that person take control. The New Testament pattern for churches is plural leadership, and that means shared leadership. If the rest of the men in leadership have relinquished the decision-making authority to one man, they have failed in their responsibility to the church and to God.[2]

The principle described above is what I call *generational leadership.*

2. Peterson, "Lessons," 174–75.

Generational Leadership

Ultimately the elders are meant to be the catalyst used by the Holy Spirit to grow healthy disciples, who become healthy leaders who, in turn, reproduce more healthy families. Elders are appointed by the Spirit to serve as the big brothers of a community; not the fathers. As the mature brothers, elders are the ones who help every member of the body discover, explore and use their giftings so they can mature into the fullness of Jesus Christ. In short, elders reproduce themselves. So then regardless of what title, or specific role an elder has in the body, his greatest goal is the development of generational leadership. Paul raised up Timothy and then Paul tells Timothy to raise up more men. Passed down to us by example of our big brother Paul, elders must mentor others to follow their example and eventually take their place.

> Those who are leaders in an assembly have to realize that they must continually nurture leadership from other men whom the Holy Spirit will raise up. A pattern can be seen in the demise of several of the assemblies which no longer exist. The initial eager leadership characteristically did not establish methods for passing leadership to the next generation. Some men seem to have been very reluctant to relinquish control as they grew old and their vigor diminished. They also do not seem to have passed their own evangelistic zeal to the next generation–only a set of rules to be followed. The vision was lost. Only a sense of duty remained for the next generation, and that is not sufficient to sustain a work of God.[3]

This basic mission, in and of itself, is an important argument for the plurality of elders in every church. The Scripture gives us a firm foundation for this goal of shared leadership that reproduces.

> The record is everywhere consistent in indicating a plurality of leadership in each church. Elders are seen in the Jewish churches of Judea in Acts 11:30 as well as the church in Jerusalem at the Jerusalem council (Acts 15:2,

3. Ibid., 175.

4, 6, 22, 23; 16:4; cf. 21:18). When Paul and Barnabas revisited the newly formed churches of South Galatia on the first missionary journey, they appointed Elders (plural) in every church (Acts 14:23). In Ephesus there was a plurality of Elders (Acts 20:17). Philippi in Europe (Macedonia) was a church with a plurality of overseers (Phil. 1:1). Titus is told by Paul to appoint Elders in every city in Crete (Tit. 1:5). James says that those who are sick are to call for the Elders (plural) of the church (singular) (James 5:14). We also see the leaders of those addressed in the book of Hebrews referred to in the plural (Heb. 13:7, 17, 24).[4]

In arguing for a plurality of elders in every church, I fear this can lead to an unholy guilt for those in a traditional pastor/CEO model. To alleviate this guilt, it is important to know that a plurality of elders is not where we begin, but where we must end.

Not a Beginning, but an End

In arguing for a plurality of elders, it must be recognized that not every church will begin with multiple pastors. Paul took several years in his first churches in Galatia to appoint elders. It took time for these future overseers to observe, and be observed, by Paul and grow into their Spirit-giftings. As months passed, the Spirit moved, and when the time was right, Paul appointed elders to lead.

There are many smaller churches today that only have one pastor (elder). Is it fair then to conclude that these churches are somehow unfaithful to God's plan? No. I would suggest to you that while the biblical ideal is a plurality of elders, there is also nothing unbiblical about having only one elder at a time. However, there is something unbiblical about an elder who is not serving as a community catalyst. Even a solo elder must raise up the younger brothers into maturity of faith. Your church may have only one elder, but the most important question is, "Is he reproducing himself?"

---

4. Fish, "Brethren Tradition," 132.

A Person; Not a Program

As to how an elder is raised and selected, there is no one "right" process for how this must be done. The emphasis, as always, is on the person whom the Spirit has called, not on developing a program that produces leaders.

> How were Elders chosen in the New Testament? The fact is that the evidence is not very clear. Paul refers in Acts 20:28 to the Holy Spirit as the one who ultimately makes a person an Elder or overseer. Theologically we could say that the Holy Spirit is the agent of Christ, the head of the Church, in appointing a person to the oversight.
>
> But how does the church recognize those whom the Holy Spirit has appointed? There are only two examples of the human involvement in the process. In Acts 14:23 Paul and Barnabas appointed Elders in those churches which they had previously established. In Titus 1:5 Paul instructs his emissary Titus to appoint Elders in every church.
>
> The only other evidence comes from the list of qualifications for Elders/overseers in 1 Timothy 3 and Titus 1. Presumably those who meet the qualifications of an Elder are to be recognized as appointed by the Holy Spirit, but nowhere is the specific process spelled out as to how the church is to do this.[5]

A Community Catalyst

My goal in this chapter is not to establish a process, but a vision for elders to become catalysts for growing the young in faith into mature brothers and sisters who themselves can become leaders who reproduce more leaders. In my own experience, I have seldom repeated the same process twice. I build and train each future leader based on where they begin and where I hope to lead them.

Yet the elder's job does not stop with reproducing individual disciples. As indicated in the diagram below, elders must develop

5. Ibid., 135–36.

deacons, and then embrace community by being active in the life of the people who make the church.

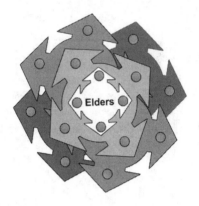

As this diagram illustrates, every elder has their own path of influence. In a larger church, this may mean participation in one of the many small groups that meet in homes. In each case the elder develops relationship with those outside of leadership and beyond the men he is mentoring. This includes a more diverse cross section of the body, but also non-believers to whom he can be a living witness. Elders do not have to be the leaders of these smaller groups, but they must be a catalyst to ensure these groups provide opportunity for every member to use their giftings and build up the church. As these smaller groups grow in maturity, the elders must again become the catalyst who leads these communities to reproduce and grow many more communities.

As we close this discussion on elders, I am struck by how important these men are to the work of the church. Are elders greater than others? No. But they are great servants who shepherd the flock along the path of maturity. I pray all who read are encouraged to serve your church with integrity and discover firsthand how elders lead a healthy family.

12

Leading with God's Vision

OVER THE PAST TWENTY years, I have been a participant in countless events focused on teaching pastors to "create" and "cast" vision. The most quoted verse has got to be Proverbs 29:18a:

"Where there is no vision, the people are unrestrained..."

Does the first half of this single verse ripped from Proverbs really provide a "biblical" foundation for all the "vision-casting" seminars, conferences and books on the market?

Two Interpretations

Vision by One Man

In nearly every case, this passage is used by pastors and other leaders to show why everyone needs to get on board with their vision. They usually say something like this...

"If we don't follow this new vision, then our church will get out of control and die."

And by "vision," most folks mean a twenty-first-century styled business plan borrowed from either secular business leaders or mega-church pastors. The idea, however, that there is one "senior" pastor or "lead" elder in charge of directing every move for the entire church is simply not in the Bible. As we have seen throughout this book, there is only one kind of biblical elder and the rest is a fiction invented by men seeking power.

Vision by One God

Alternatively, we can take this passage from Proverbs in its full context and allow God to direct our path. First, the translation from the NIV:

> Where there is no revelation, people cast off restraint;
> but blessed is the one who heeds wisdom's instruction.
> (Prov 29:18 NIV11)

And another from the ESV:

> Where there is no prophetic vision the people cast off restraint, but blessed is he who keeps the law. (Prov 29:18 ESV)

"Vision" then is not the dreams of one man at the helm to build a church, but a prayerful consent by the elders to follow the revelation of God. When we abandon God's vision for man's business plans, we will perish . . . and we are perishing . . .

One Vision for Every Body

So then, what is God's one vision for his church?

First, grow in holiness: God's vision (revelation) is that we proclaim the gospel to the lost, that we, the church, love one another and lead one another to grow in holiness. My friend Alan Knox summarizes it this way:

> The idea that God presents his vision for a group's service through a single individual (i.e., a pastor) is not found in the New Testament. There is no indication by the NT writers that a pastor or Elder or other leader is responsible for telling a group of people how to serve God and others.
>
> Even when Paul presented his own life and service to the gospel as an example to others, he did not tell them

exactly how to serve God for themselves. Instead, Paul clearly tells his readers that through God's grace each of his readers are given gifts, opportunities, and ability to serve God through serving one another and others in different ways. As Paul followed the Holy Spirit in serving others, he expected others to follow the Spirit as well.[1]

Second, live for eternity: We grow in holiness in anticipation of Christ's return and the knowledge that one day we will be in eternity with him. Chris Brauns writes this:

> One of the most compelling leadership vision statements ever written is found in Revelation 22. Writing to a suffering church, John shares a vision of where God's people are headed: a heavenly city with a river flowing from the throne, surrounded by trees with people from every tribe and tongue.
>
> We often tell our children at home, "I can't promise you that I will always be around. We live in a world of cancer and accidents. But if for some reason we get separated then we'll meet on the other side."[2]

We, the church, can no longer accept the "follow one man's vision" distortion of the Scripture! There are not *many* "visions" for different churches. There is only one Lord, one faith, one baptism, and one vision for the one church.

In seeing that there is only one vision, I think it is important to transition our discussion into the role of the elder's wife in contrast to the often crushing expectations placed upon her in the pastor as CEO model.

---

1. Knox, "Where There Is No Vision."
2. Braums, "Church Leaders Must Cast Vision."

13

The Elder's Wife in Community

I AM BLESSED BY God with an amazing wife who not only supports my call to serve the church, but who herself has a great call upon her life. Suzanne is a strong leader, faithful disciple-maker, great partner, and I could not be the man I am today without her love. But this is more than just a glowing endorsement of my wife, it is my way of introducing this chapter on what it means to be an elder's wife. The role of an "elder's wife" is much different than the role of a "pastor's wife." Over the past few decades, my wife has served in both roles so she understands the good and bad of ministry. What follows is Suzanne's take on why being an elder's wife can be such a blessing.

∼

I love being the wife of a husband who dedicates his time and talents to the church ministry and the kingdom of God. I wanted to marry a pastor at a very young age and now I am living out that desire every day. I have been in this ministry role for almost twenty years and love it.

In our last two church plants, my husband built the leadership around a plurality of elders. This approach to shared leadership has given me a unique role as an elder's wife as opposed to a senior pastor's wife. I am thankful for God's calling on my life because I know many women who are married to senior pastors and they struggle daily with a variety of issues.

Never Alone

When there is only one senior pastor, there can only be one senior pastor's wife. This role makes a woman feel like no other woman in the congregation can truly understand the pressures and struggles she faces. This sense of isolation often leads to a lack of meaningful friendships within the church. Who can the pastor's wife talk to about her marital struggles? Who can she confide in about the challenge of being a mom? There is a constant concern that any sign of "weakness" will come back to hurt her husband's ability to lead the church.

When teamed with another elder's wife, there is no isolation. As an elder's wife, I always have somebody by my side and I no longer feel alone in ministry. An elder's wife can develop deeper friendships with other wives—a safe friend in their life to talk to about personal issues as well as ministry dilemmas. My fellow elder's wife is becoming one of my best friends! Sadly, many pastors' wives have very few friends in the church. It can be very difficult to trust and confide in people, but I can now truly experience the beauty of friendship as an elder's wife.

Feeling Free

For decades the church has put tremendous pressure on a senior pastor's wife to perform. Whether it be to play the piano, lead a Bible study or speak at a ladies' retreat. But what if she doesn't feel comfortable doing these things? There can be an unspoken expectation to perform in these areas even if it isn't her calling. Even when a pastor candidates for a job, committees often see the pastor's wife as a "free" hire . . . someone who will put in the hours of work without any pay.

Pastors' wives often feel like they are not doing enough for the church. Some pastors' wives don't feel called to be in ministry and yet people make them feel like they should be and accuse them for not doing enough for the church. Unrealistic expectations are probably one of the hardest things as a pastor's wife. This is probably the leading cause of the stress that can be developed.

In the early years of my ministry, I didn't enjoy speaking in public. Now twenty years later, God has developed that skill in my life and I love it. However, the pressure I felt when I was younger was difficult. We can agree that every follower of Christ is growing and maturing in Christ at different speeds and the same is true for pastors' wives. Yet, the church puts pressure on a senior pastor's wife to be excellent at all these things at all times.

Because I am part of a team of elders' wives, the pressure is off so I can focus on my spiritual giftings rather then trying to be everything to everyone. As an elder's wife, there is no pressure to perform as a solo act and more support to serve in a community of leaders. Having a friend who is in your corner, someone who has your back, can bring such freedom. Sometimes pastors' wives feel like they are supposed to be the "first lady" of the church. This is very unfortunate because it can be avoided when the focus is a team approach to ministry rather than an individual approach.

Emotionally Supported

People leave church for many different reasons. One reason can certainly be because of a conflict with the senior pastor. As women, this can be emotionally difficult when someone leaves because they are angry or upset with our husband. We love our husbands and we feel responsible. The pastor's wife feels responsible to make sure everyone is happy and any kind of discord can leave us feeling unsettled and frustrated. We can feel responsible for meeting people's needs and desires. Even though we know it is not right, as women, we are emotionally charged. A senior pastor's wife can put undue responsibility on her life that she has no control over.

Having shared leadership within the church takes the pressure off the "one man" to be responsible for everything. The same feeling of support goes for the elder's wife. If people leave the church, the burden doesn't rely solely on one woman's shoulders. As women, it can be emotionally difficult to see people leave, but being a part of a team can make the struggle more manageable. As the wife of an elder, there is less reason to feel the burden of responsibility and more support from the community of wives.

Secure in Myself

An attack on the church is an attack on the pastor and this can leave me, as a wife, feeling very defensive. It's human nature to defend the people we love. It is easy, but not always healthy, for a wife to defend every action and decision made by her husband. It is understandable because when the church leadership is structured solely around the senior pastor, this naturally can put the senior pastor's wife in a difficult place of being his only real supporter.

It can be very difficult to have people upset at your husband, especially when you know how hard they are working for the church. Bitterness and resentment can set in toward people who demonstrate this kind of animosity. However, when you have the emotional support of other elders' wives, it can ease the pain of these types of situations. I also know that because my husband is not making every decision alone, it is not left to me to defend everything he does. He already has built in support, so I am able to be a better source of both encouragement and accountability. Freed from being my husband's sole defender, I am able to be a better sounding board for ideas. This makes me a better wife and gives me the security I need to be a better ministry partner.

Protected by Community

A senior pastor's wife often feels like she lives in a glass house. People in the church are constantly watching and judging. People, without realizing it, are scrutinizing what she eats, how she parents, how her children behave, what her husband preached and the list goes on and on. Sadly, a senior pastor's wife is often left feeling inadequate and insecure.

The pastor's wife can often feel judged and criticized—as many Christians do. Having the support of another elder's wife can help lighten the blow and bring perspective and encouragement. There are times when I need other women who understand me, and now I have a built in support system among the other elders' wives.

At the end of the day, I am very thankful for my role as elder's wife. I am thankful to be a part of an elders' wife team that has a mission to reach people for Jesus and shepherd the flock that has been entrusted to us. I am thankful to be an elder's wife because I never lead alone—I always lead in community.

14

The Future of Eldership

As you may recall from the introduction, Steve was the senior pastor of a big church, but he felt like a failure. He felt alone and needed a change. Sitting across the table, I shared with Steve the vision for shared leadership outlined in this book. I let him know how he could transition his church from a pastor as CEO model into a plurality of elders. I promised to stand by Steve and help him change the culture so he would no longer be tired and burned out. He left our meeting excited for the future, but his joy did not last long.

Sadly, just a few days later, Steve called me and said that while he wanted to make the changes we talked about, "now is just not the right time." Steve desperately needed the change, but was convinced by the voices in his life that transitioning the church leadership toward a plurality of elders would make him a failure as a pastor. Steve's dad was a pastor of a mega-church, his mentor of twenty years was a mega-church pastor, Steve's brothers were successful business leaders . . . all of Steve's role modes, all the books Steve read, and all the Christian magazines celebrating the mega-pastor told him to suck it up and stick it out as a CEO. Everything in Steve wanted to change—he needed to change—but the dearth of churches modeling shared leadership led him to conclude that change was impossible. He felt trapped with no way out.

More troubling than Steve's dilemma, is the dilemma of many young leaders who dream of serving with a team of elders, but don't see a way in. Joseph Hellerman summarizes the challenge this way:

> Paul's vision for authentic Christian leadership is a case in point. The concept of a team of pastors, whose leadership arises naturally out of mutually edifying peer relationships, will not even be on the radar screen of most churches looking to hire recent seminary graduates.[1]

This quote above is painfully true . . . I know because I've lived it. For several years after leaving my first church plant I felt disenfranchised and alienated from most churches and had begun to wonder if I would ever shepherd another congregation . . . I just didn't know if there is a place left for me in the American church. But fortunately for me, Hellerman also shares in his own story of leadership and I was encouraged to not give up.

This book on elders has come at a price. It is the result of many tough years of learning to trust in Scripture above the demands of culture. Through time, I have come to believe that the future of church is found in our past. Slowly we are coming to embrace the biblical ideal that every follower of Jesus is a priest and therefore called to mature into a role of leadership.

> For this reason our fathers devoutly spoke of an office of all believers. In Christ's Church there are not merely a few officials and a mass of idle, unworthy subjects, but every believer has a calling, a task, a vital charge. And inasmuch as we are convinced that we perform the task because the King has laid it upon us not for ourselves, nor even from the motive of philanthropy, but to serve the Church, to this extent has our work an official character, altho the world denies us the honor.[2]

The world does not recognize God's system of leadership, and for too long we have allowed the convictions of the world to

---

1. Hellerman, *Embracing Shared Ministry*, 353.
2. Kuyper, *Work of the Holy Spirit*, 183.

determine the structure of our churches. The recent post-modern shift in culture has allowed some churches to change gears from a system of hierarchical leadership (focused on one man) to a team model (focused on Christ and mission). Yet experience demonstrates that the future of church leadership will not come easily.

The Future in Transition

A few years back, *Leadership Journal* did an exposé on The Next Level Church (TNL) in Denver, Colorado.[3] TNL began with a team/elder approach but soon gave in to the pressures of the status quo and elevated one man above the others to the role of senior pastor. After some amazing years of massive growth, TNL lost their senior pastor to sin. But instead of replacing him with another senior pastor, TNL's leadership decided to embrace their original vision for shared (elder) leadership. In the article, Brian Gray says the following:

> I wasn't at TNL during that crisis, but I also saw a senior pastor model entirely fall apart at my previous church. It got really bad. I began thinking there had to be a better way to do church. There is something systemically unhealthy about becoming dependent upon a single leader.[4]

As churches seek to modify their leadership structures, many hurdles will arise. Change will require a new mind-set that seeks to protect our leaders instead of setting them up to fail. John Miller offers the following lesson:

> In our case, we did put too many responsibilities and burdens on our senior pastor—a lot more than one guy should handle. We made him the public face of TNL. He was the go-to guy for everything. And the rest of us were okay with that because we liked being in the background and not having to bear the burden of making it

3. Jethani, "Next & Level."
4. Ibid.

all happen. But in the end, it was unfair to him and it was unfair to the church.[5]

As I have shared throughout this book, a return to Scripture will require that we look outside our culture and into the history of the early church, but experience informs us that transitioning to a plurality of elders is "the most important step"[6] in strengthening the local church.

Over the past several years, I have observed and counseled with several churches making this transition from a senior pastor to a plurality of elders. More work needs to be done in helping churches transition to a plurality of elders, and when that work is done I am convinced that many more churches will follow. As we prepare for the future, there are two trends to keep watching.

The Future of Vocation

The economy and the culture of the West is changing. Study after study indicates that the coming generations have less interest in organized church . . . or at least church as it exists today. If these trends continue, there will be less disposable income and fewer opportunities for pastors to make their living in full-time ministry. For the elders at Reunion Church, our response has been to make a living outside the church and not rely on the tithes of the congregation for a full-time salary. So while we do not have as much time to spend doing ministry, it forces us to work as a team, rely on one another to accomplish our goals, and ultimately being intentionally bi-vocational insulates our church from an unstable economy. Together, we are experiencing, exploring and encouraging others to discover the beauty of bi-vocational ministry.

5. Ibid.

6. Newton and Schmucker, "Elders in the Life of the Church," 176.

The Future Overseas

One of the hurdles to church planting overseas is that a model that relies on the pastor getting a full-time salary is hard to replicate in poorer nations. At our church, we are working with potential planters to adopt a plurality model that relies on tent-making teams. More time, research, and study needs to be done in this area, but it is our hope that we can advance the gospel by planting more self-sustaining churches in poorer nations.

In addressing the challenge of vocation and overseas planting, our hope is to inspire the next generation of Christians to see a way forward with a new kind of leadership where elders lead a healthy family.

The Future of Multiethnic

From beginning to end, God's ideal has been to create a family representing every nation, every tribe and every tongue. From YHWH's covenant with Abraham (Gen 12:1–2), to Jesus' commissioning of the disciples (Matt 28:18–20), through Paul's encouragement to the church (Gal 3:21–22), toward the final promise of eternal life (Rev 7:9), God has given us a powerful dream that all people from every ethnic and social status should worship him together in equality. Yet to build diversity, the local church must model diversity. There are some churches leading by example and paving the way by building strong multiethnic leadership teams, and the hope of our church is to become a place of reunion that advances God's dream of diversity through a plurality elders who represent the community we seek to reach with the gospel. We seek to be a diverse eldership that allows each man to share the call to lead in perfect equality and model the unity of the Spirit to our broken world.

Bibliography

Averbeck, Richard E. "The Focus of Baptism in the New Testament." *Grace Theological Journal* 2 (1981) 265–301.

Bailey, Kenneth E. "Women in the New Testament: A Middle Eastern Cultural View." *Evangelical Review of Theology* 22 (1998) 208–26. Reprinted from *Anvil* 11 (1994) 7–24. Logos Bible Software.

Barton, George Aaron. "Salutations." In *Encyclopædia of Religion and Ethics*, edited by James Hastings et al. New York: Scribner, 1908–1926.

Bates, Carrie L. "Gender Ontology and Women in Ministry in the Early Church." *Priscilla Papers* 25 (2011) 6–12. Logos Bible Software.

Baxter, Richard. *The Reformed Pastor.* Edited by William Brown. (1882:1994) Escondido, CA, Ephesians 4 Group, el. ed., Logos Bible Software.

Beach, Nancy. "Women in Church Leadership—Disappointed but Not Desparing." Slingshot Group. http://slingshotgroup.org/women.

Black, Robert, and Ronald McClung. *1 & 2 Timothy, Titus, Philemon: A Commentary for Bible Students.* Indianapolis: Wesleyan, 2004.

Braums, Chris. "Church Leaders Must Cast Vision: 'Where There Is No Vision the People Perish' Revisited." *A Brick in the Valley* (blog). June 19, 2012. http://www.chrisbrauns.com/2012/06/church-leaders-must-cast-vision-where-there-is-no-vision-the-people-perish-revisited.

Brown, John. *Analytical Exposition of the Epistle of Paul the Apostle to the Romans.* Edinburgh, 1857.

Burleson, Wade. "Our Problem Is Authoritarianism and Not Legalism." Istoria Ministries blog. January 26, 2012. http://www.wadeburleson.org/2012/01/our-problem-is-authoritarianism-and-not.html.

Buswell, James, Jr. "Notes and Reflections on the Alleged Genetic Relationship between Christianity and Ancient Contemporaneous Religions." *Bibliotheca Sacra* 81 (1924) 418–39.

Campbell, R. Alastair. *The Elders: Seniority within Earliest Christianity.* London: T. & T. Clark, 2004.

————. "The Elders: Seniority in Earliest Christianity." *Tyndale Bulletin* 44 (1993) 183–87.

Charteris, A. H. "Woman's Work in the Church." *Presbyterian Review* 9 (1888) 33–36.

Cohn-Sherbok, Dan. *Voices of Messianic Judaism: Confronting Critical Issues Facing a Maturing Movement*. Baltimore: Messianic Jewish, 2001.

Decker, Rodney J. "Polity and the Elder Issue." *Grace Theological Journal* 9 (1988) 257–77.

DeMoss, Nancy Leigh, and Mary A. Kassian. *True Woman 101: Divine Design; An Eight-Week Study on Biblical Womanhood*. Chicago: Moody, 2012. Kindle ed.

Duling, Dennis C. *A Marginal Scribe: Studies of the Gospel of Matthew in Social-Scientific Perspective*. Matrix: The Bible in Mediterranean Context 7. Eugene, OR: Cascade, 2012.

Dunnam, Maxie D., et al. *Mastering Personal Growth*. Sisters, OR: Multnomah, 1992.

Elwell, Walter A., ed. *Evangelical Dictionary of Biblical Theology*. Grand Rapids: Baker, 1997. Logos Bible Software.

Estep, William R. *The Anabaptist Story: An Introduction to Sixteenth-Century Anabaptism*. 3rd ed. Grand Rapids: Eerdmans, 1996.

Fish, John H., III. "Brethren Tradition or New Testament Church Truth." *Emmaus Journal* 2 (1993) 111–53.

Freedman, David Noel, et al., eds. *The Anchor Yale Bible Dictionary*. New York: Doubleday, 1992.

Galli, Mark, and Ted Olsen. *131 Christians Everyone Should Know*. Nashville: Broadman & Holman, 2000.

Glasscock, Ed. "The Biblical Concept of Elder." *Bibliotheca Sacra* 144 (1987) 66–78.

————. "The Husband of One Wife: Requirement in 1 Timothy 3:2." In *Vital Biblical Issues: Examining Problem Passages of the Bible*, edited by Roy B. Zuck, 187–99. Grand Rapids: Kregel, 1994.

Goble, Roy. "Leadership as a Code Word for Power." Red Letter Christians. September 13, 2012. http://www.redletterchristians.org/leadership-as-a-code-word-for-power.

Gray, James Comper. *Biblical Encyclopedia and Museum*. Vol. 13. Hartford, CT: Scranton, 1900.

Grudem, W. A. *Systematic Theology: An Introduction to Biblical Doctrine*. Grand Rapids: Zondervan, 1994.

Guinness, Os. *Dining with the Devil: The Megachurch Movement Flirts with Modernity*. Grand Rapids: Baker, 1993.

Hastings, James, et al. *Dictionary of the Bible*. New York: Scribner, 1909.

Hayes, Edward L. "The Call to Ministry." *Bibliotheca Sacra* 157 (2000) 88–98.

Hellerman, Joseph H. *Embracing Shared Ministry: Power & Authority in the Early Church and Why It Matters Today*. Grand Rapids: Kregel, 2013.

Henry, Carl F. H. *God, Revelation, and Authority.* Vol. 6. Wheaton, IL: Crossway, 1999.

Hodge, Charles, ed. "Review of Theories of the Eldership." *Biblical Repertory and Princeton Review* 32 (1860) 185–236.

Hoehner, Harold W. "Can a Woman Be a Pastor-Teacher?" *Journal of the Evangelical Theological Society* 50 (2007) 759–71.

Hort, Fenton John Anthony. *The Christian Ecclesia: A Course of Lectures on the Early History and Early Conception of the Ecclesia.* London: Macmillan, 1914.

Hugenberger, Gordon P. "Women In Church Office: Hermeneutics or Exegesis? A Survey of Approaches to 1 Tim 2:8–15." *Journal of the Evangelical Theological Society* 35 (1992) 340–59.

Hunt, Sunsan. "The Seasons of a Woman's Life: When She's Through Mothering, Will Her Life Seem Over?" *Journal for Biblical Manhood and Womanhood* 5 (2000) 8–9.

Jackson, Thomas A. "Concerning Spiritual Gifts: A Study of I Corinthians 12." *Faith and Mission* 7 (1989) 59–68.

Jackson, Samuel Macauley, ed. *The New Schaff-Herzog Encyclopedia of Religious Knowledge: Embracing Biblical, Historical, Doctrinal, and Practical Theology and Biblical, Theological, and Ecclesiastical Biography from the Earliest Times to the Present Day.* New York: Funk & Wagnalls, 1908–1914.

Jelinek, John A. "Annotations on the Text and Message of 1 Timothy 2:1–15." *Journal of Ministry and Theology* 2 (1998) 162–88.

Jethani, Skye. "Next & Level." *Leadership Journal,* spring 2008. http://www.christianitytoday.com/le/2008/spring/3.24.html.

Jones, Peyton. *Church Zero: Raising 1st Century Churches out of the Ashes of the 21st Century Church.* Colorado Springs: Cook, 2013.

Keener, Craig S. *The IVP Bible Background Commentary: New Testament.* Downers Grove: InterVarsity, 1993.

Kittel, Gerhard, et al., eds. *Theological Dictionary of the New Testament.* Vol. 6. Grand Rapids: Eerdmans, 1964–1976. Logos Bible Software.

Knox, Alan. "The Vocational Pastor: Examine All the Evidence." *The Assembling of the Church* (blog). June 8, 2012. http://www.alanknox.net/2012/06/the-vocational-pastor-examine-all-the-evidence.

———. "Where There Is No Vision, the People Perish." *The Assembling of the Church* (blog). October 5, 2011. http://www.alanknox.net/2011/10/where-there-is-no-vision-the-people-perish.

Kuyper, Abraham. *The Work of the Holy Spirit.* New York: Funk & Wagnalls, 1900.

Lewis, Robert M. "The 'Women' of 1 Timothy 3:11." In *Vital New Testament Issues: Examining New Testament Passages and Problems,* edited by Roy B. Zuck, 188–95. Grand Rapids: Kregel, 1996.

Lightfoot, John. *The Whole Works of the Rev. John Lightfoot.* Edited by John Rogers Pitman. Vol. 5. London, 1822.

MacLeod, David J. "The Primacy of Scripture and the Church." *Emmaus Journal* 6 (1997) 43–96.

Mappes, David A. "The 'Elder' in the Old and New Testaments." *Bibliotheca Sacra* 154 (1997) 80–92.

———. "The 'Elder' in the Old and New Testaments." In *Vital Church Issues: Examining Principles and Practices in Church Leadership*, edited by Roy B. Zuck, 75–81. Grand Rapids: Kregel, 1998.

———. "The New Testament Elder, Overseer, and Pastor." In *Vital Church Issues: Examining Principles and Practices in Church Leadership*, edited by Roy B. Zuck, 82–88. Grand Rapids: Kregel, 1998.

Meisinger, George E. "Elders: How Many?" *Chafer Theological Seminary Journal* 10 (2004) 10–26.

Merkle, Benjamin. *40 Questions about Elders and Deacons*. 40 Questions & Answers Series. Grand Rapids: Kregel, 2008. Kindle ed.

———. *Why Elders? A Biblical and Practical Guide for Church Members*. Grand Rapids: Kregel, 2009. Kindle ed.

Metaxas, Eric. *Bonhoeffer: Pastor, Martyr, Prophet, Spy*. Nashville: Nelson, 2010. Logos Bible Software.

Miller, David W. "The Uniqueness of the New Testament Church Eldership." *Grace Theological Journal* 6 (1985) 315–27.

Miller, J. R. "Algebra in the Church." *More than Cake* (blog). July 27, 2012. http://www.morethancake.org/archives/2339.

———. "Blind Foxes & Velvet Fences." *More than Cake* (blog). August 2, 2012. http://www.morethancake.org/archives/685.

———. "Every Follower a Leader." *More than Cake* (blog). July 16, 2012. http://www.morethancake.org/archives/2284.

———. "Feminism, the Organic Church, and Deprecation of Leadership." *More than Cake* (blog). September 18, 2012. http://www.morethancake.org/archives/1133.

———. "Paparazzi Pastors Leading a Celebrity Church." *More than Cake* (blog). February 23, 2012. http://www.morethancake.org/archives/987.

———. *Promise of the Father: Healing the Christian Legacy of Segregation and Denominationalism*. Emerging Life, 2008. Logos Bible Software.

———. "Video Training for Preaching the Word in a Post-Modern World." *More than Cake* (blog). June 7, 2012. http://www.morethancake.org/archives/1932.

———. "Women and the Pastoral Gift." *More than Cake* (blog). December 19, 2012. http://www.morethancake.org/archives/5087.

Morey, Robert A. *The Encyclopedia of Practical Christianity*. Las Vegas: Christian Scholars, 2004.

Mounce, William D. *Pastoral Epistles*. Word Biblical Commentary 46. Dallas: Word, 2000.

Newton, Paul A., and Matt Schmucker. *Elders in the Life of the Church: Rediscovering the Biblical Model for Church Leadership*. Grand Rapids: Kregel, 2014.